BARACK OBAMA

A POCKET BIOGRAPHY OF

OUR 44TH PRESIDENT

S ... E N

INTRODUCTION BY

HENRY LOUIS GATES JR.

OXFORD
UNIVERSITY PRESS

2009

OXFORD
UNIVERSITY PRESS

OXFORD NEW YORK

Auckland Cape Town Dar es Salaam Hong Kong Karachi
Kuala Lumpur Madrid Melbourne Mexico City Nairobi
New Delhi Shanghai Taipei Toronto

WITH OFFICES IN

Argentina Austria Brazil Chile Czech Republic France Greece
Guatemala Hungary Italy Japan Poland Portugal Singapore
South Korea Switzerland Thailand Turkey Ukraine Vietnam

Copyright © 2009 by Oxford University Press

Published by Oxford University Press, Inc.
198 Madison Avenue, New York, NY 10016
www.oup.com

Oxford is a registered trademark of Oxford University Press

Library of Congress Cataloging-in-Publication Data

Niven, Steven J.
Barack Obama : a pocket biography /
Steven J. Niven ; introduction by Henry Louis Gates, Jr.
p. cm.
Includes bibliographical references.
Summary: "A pocket guide on Barack Hussein Obama, the 44th president of
the United States of America. Provides biographical information on Obama, his
"A More Perfect Union" speech, and an introduction about African Americans and
politics by Henry Louis Gates Jr.]"—Provided by publisher.
ISBN 978-0-19-539078-0
1. Obama, Barack. 2. United States—Politics and government—2001- 3.
Presidents—United States—Election—2008. 4. Political campaigns—United
States—History—21st century. 5. Presidents—United States—Biography. 6.
Legislators—United States—Biography. 7. African American legislators—
Biography. 8. United States. Congress. Senate—Biography. 9. Racially mixed
people—United States—Biography. I. Title.
E908.N58 2009
973.932092—dc22
[B]
2008049451

1 3 5 7 9 8 6 4 2

Printed in the United States of America on acid-free paper

★ ★ ★ ★

CONTENTS

FOR MAM AND DAD
KIRSTEN, ANYA, AND ZIGGY

★ ★ ★ ★

ACKNOWLEDGMENTS

I very much doubt that I would ever have published a book on Barack Obama, had it not been for Evelyn Brooks Higginbotham. When I was an exchange student at the University of Pennsylvania in the 1980s, she encouraged me to be a historian and allowed me to see that I might best understand America by first understanding how African Americans shaped that country's history. As a researcher for the late A. Leon Higginbotham, I came to see how the law first cemented and later subverted the color line in America. I also owe a great debt to Owen Dudley Edwards of the University of Edinburgh; William Leuchtenburg and Joel Williamson of the University of North Carolina; and John Bollard, Editorial Director of the Native American Biography Project. They made me a better thinker and a better writer.

As a writer and executive editor on the *African American National Biography*, I have learned much from my editors in chief, Henry Louis Gates Jr. and Evelyn Higginbotham, and from my colleagues in that long and worthy endeavor: Tony Aiello at Oxford University Press, who first approached me about doing this biography, John Bollard, Martin Coleman, Sol Levy, Lisa Rivo, Kate Tuttle, Tom Wolejko, Julie Wolf, and Donald Yacovone. For this essay, Mark LaFlaur provided invaluable editing.

This book is dedicated to my mam and dad, Jean Niven and William George Niven, and to my wife, Kirsten Condry, for her love, encouragement, and valuable advice on this essay and for the past 8 years. It is also for our infant son, Ziggy (John) and three-year-old daughter, Anya, who will both grow up never having known a time when American presidents were only white. In fact, other than *Sesame Street* characters, Anya recognizes only one person on television: Barack Obama. "He's the President."

Steven J. Niven
SCOTTSVILLE, NEW YORK

INTRODUCTION

HENRY LOUIS GATES JR.

We have all heard stories about those few magical transformative moments in African American history, extraordinary ritual occasions through which the geographically and socially diverse black community—a nation within a nation, really—molds itself into one united body, determined to achieve one great social purpose and to bear witness to the process by which this grand achievement occurs.

The first time was New Year's Day in 1863, when tens of thousands of black people huddled together all over the North waiting to see if Abraham Lincoln would sign the Emancipation Proclamation. The second was the night of 22 June 1938, the storied rematch between Joe Louis and Max Schmeling, when black families and friends crowded around radios to listen and cheer as the Brown Bomber knocked out Schmeling in the first round. The third, of course, was 28 August 1963, when the Rev. Dr. Martin Luther King Jr. proclaimed to the world that he had a dream, in the shadow of a brooding Lincoln, peering down on the assembled throng, while those of us who couldn't be with him in Washington sat around our black-and-white television sets, bound together by King's melodious voice through our tears and with quickened flesh.

But we have never seen anything like we witnessed last night. Nothing could have prepared any of us for the eruption (and, yes, that is the word) of spontaneous celebration that manifested itself in black homes, gathering places, and the streets of our communities when Sen. Barack Obama was declared President-elect Obama. From Harlem to Harvard, from Maine to Hawaii—and even Alaska—from "the prodigious hilltops of New Hampshire . . . [to] Stone Mountain of Georgia," as Dr. King put it, each of us will always remember this moment, as will our children, whom we woke up to watch history being made.

My colleagues and I laughed and shouted, whooped and hollered, hugged each other and cried. My father waited ninety-five years to see this day happen, and when he called last night, I silently thanked God for allowing him to live long enough to cast his vote for the first black man to become president. And even he still can't quite believe it!

★

How many of our ancestors have given their lives—how many millions of slaves toiled in the fields in endlessly thankless and mindless labor—before this generation could live to see a black person become president? "How long, Lord?" the spiritual goes; "not long!" is the resounding response. What would Frederick Douglass and W. E. B. Du Bois say if they could know what our people had at long last achieved? What would Sojourner Truth and Harriet Tubman say? What would Dr. King himself say? Would they say that all those lost hours of brutalizing toil and labor leading to spent, half-fulfilled lives, all those humiliations that our ancestors had to suffer through each and every day, all those slights and rebuffs and recriminations, all those rapes and murders, lynchings and assassinations, all those Jim Crow laws and protest marches, those snarling dogs and bone-breaking water hoses, all of those beatings and all of those killings, all of those collective dreams deferred—that the unbearable pain of all of those tragedies had, in the end, been assuaged at least somewhat through Barack Obama's election? This certainly doesn't wipe that bloody slate clean. His victory is not redemption for all of this suffering; rather, it is the symbolic culmination of the black freedom struggle, the grand achievement of a great, collective dream. Would they say that surviving these horrors, hope against hope, was the price we had to pay to become truly free, to live to see—exactly 389 years after the first African slaves landed on these shores—that "great gettin' up morning," on 4 November 2008, when a black man—Barack Hussein Obama—was elected the first African American president of the United States?

I think they would, resoundingly and with one voice proclaim, "Yes! Yes! And yes, again!" I believe they would tell us that it had been worth the price that we, collectively, have had to pay—the price of President-elect Obama's ticket.

★

When James Earl Jones became America's first black fictional president in the 1972 film, *The Man*, I remember thinking, "imagine that!" His character, Douglass Dilman, the president pro tempore of the Senate, ascends to the presidency after the president and the speaker of the House are killed in a building collapse, and after the vice president declines the office due to advanced age and ill health. A fantasy if ever there was one, we thought. But that year, life would imitate art: Congresswoman Shirley Chisholm attempted to transform *The Man* into *The Woman*, when she became the first black woman to run for president in the Democratic Party. She received 152 first-ballot votes at the 1972 Democratic National Convention. Then in 1988 Jesse Jackson got 1,219 delegate votes at the Democratic convention, 29 percent of the total, coming in second only to the nominee, Michael Dukakis.

The award for prescience, however, goes to Jacob K. Javits, the liberal Republican senator from New York who, incredibly, just a year after the integration of Central High School in Little Rock, predicted that the first black president would be elected in the year 2000. In an essay titled "Integration from the Top Down" printed in *Esquire* magazine in 1958, he wrote:

"What manner of man will this be, this possible Negro Presidential candidate of 2000? Undoubtedly, he will be well-educated. He will be well-traveled and have a keen grasp of his country's role in the world and its relationships. He will be a dedicated internationalist with working comprehension of the intricacies of foreign aid, technical assistance and reciprocal trade. . . . Assuredly, though, despite his other characteristics, he will have developed the fortitude to withstand the vicious smear attacks that came his way as he fought to the top in government and politics . . . those in the vanguard may expect to be the targets for scurrilous attacks, as the hate mongers, in the last ditch efforts, spew their verbal and written poison."

In the same essay, Javits predicted both the election of a black senator and the appointment of the first black Supreme Court justice by 1968. Edward Brooke was elected to the Senate by Massachusetts voters in 1966. Thurgood Marshall was confirmed in 1967. Javits also predicted the election to the House of Representatives of "between thirty and forty qualified Negroes" in the 106th Congress in 2000. In fact, thirty-seven black U.S. representatives, among them fourteen women, were elected that year.

All in all, Sen. Javits was one very keen prognosticator. And when we reflect upon the characteristics that Javits insisted the first black president must possess—he must be well-educated, well-traveled, have a keen grasp of his country's role in the world, be a dedicated internationalist and have a very thick skin—it is astonishing how accurately he is describing the background and character of Barack Obama.

So what does Barack Obama's election portend for the future of race relations in America, and for African Americans in particular? I wish we could say that Barack Obama's election will magically reduce the number of teenage pregnancies or the level of drug addiction in the black community. I wish we could say that what happened last night will suddenly make black children learn to read and write as if their lives depended on it, and that their high school completion rates will become the best in the country. I wish we could say that these things are about to happen, but I doubt that they will.

But there is one thing we can proclaim today, without question: that the election of Barack Obama as president of the United States of America means that "The Ultimate Color Line," as the subtitle of Javits' *Esquire* essay put it, has at long last been crossed. It has been crossed by our very first postmodern Race Man, a man who embraces his African cultural and genetic heritage so securely that he can transcend it, becoming the candidate of choice to tens of millions of Americans who do not look like him.

How does that make me feel? Like I've always imagined my father and his friends felt back in 1938, on the day that Joe Louis knocked out Max Schmeling. But ten thousand times better than that. All I can say is "Amazing Grace! How sweet the sound."

THE AMERICAN CANDIDATE

BARACK OBAMA'S PATH TO THE PRESIDENCY

AMERICA 1961

Barack Hussein Obama Jr., the first African American president of the United States, was born in Honolulu, Hawaii, on August 4, 1961. His birth coincided with a crucial turning point in the history of American race relations, although like many turning points it did not seem so at the time. Few observers believed that Jim Crow was in its death throes. Seven years after the Supreme Court's landmark school desegregation ruling, *Brown v. Board of Education* (1954), less than one percent of black schoolchildren in the South attended integrated public schools. At the undergraduate level, the University of North Carolina at Chapel Hill was one of the few integrated southern colleges, having admitted three black students in 1955. By 1960 that number had risen—to four. In 1961, Charlayne Hunter and Hamilton Holmes successfully integrated the University of Georgia, but most other major southern colleges, including Duke, Clemson, and the flagship state universities of South Carolina, Alabama, and Mississippi remained segregated. Despite the lack of de jure segregation, northern universities were only marginally better. At Columbia University near Harlem in New York City, where Obama would graduate with a BA in 1983, and which in the 1920s had educated the writers Langston Hughes and Zora Neale Hurston and the singer, actor, and activist Paul Robeson, only five African Americans were enrolled in 1960. Obama's other *alma mater*, Harvard Law School, graduated its first African American, George L. Ruffin, in 1869, but nearly a century later, there were rarely more than two or three blacks in each graduating class, and there were no African Americans on the Harvard Law School faculty until 1969.

As in education, the color line in American politics remained fairly rigid in 1961. Despite the Civil Rights acts of 1957 and 1960 and promises from the new administration of President John F. Kennedy, in some Black Belt counties of Georgia, Mississippi, Alabama, and Louisiana, up to 90 percent of African Americans were excluded from the political process, as they had been by state law and custom since the late nineteenth century. There were a handful of black state legislators and city councilmen in the North, and a sprinkling of African Americans sat on boards of education and city councils in the urban upper South, but there were no black mayors other than in all-black towns. While ten percent of all Americans were black in the 1960 census, only four African Americans served in the 435-member House of Representatives. All were Democrats representing large northern cities; only one of them chaired a major committee, New York's Adam Clayton Powell Jr., who oversaw the Education and Labor Committee. No African Americans sat in the hundred-member U.S. Senate between the departure of Blanche K. Bruce (R-MS) in 1881 and the arrival of Edward W. Brooke (R-MA) in 1967. No African Americans served in President John F. Kennedy's cabinet, and none had served in the cabinets of any previous administration. The federal judiciary, the branch of government most responsive to black demands for equality, offered a slightly more positive picture. In the fall of 1961, the U.S. Senate confirmed James B. Parsons of Chicago as the nation's second and Wade McCree of Detroit as the third African American federal judges. Segregationist resistance in the Senate Judiciary Committee would prevent another Kennedy appointee, NAACP chief counsel, Thurgood Marshall, from joining them on the federal bench until 1962.

By August 1961, however, there was also an emerging challenge to the old racial order—at least in the South. Indeed, in the very week of Obama's birth, Robert P. "Bob" Moses, a young black New Yorker who had been influenced by the grassroots community organizer Ella Baker, the pacifist Bayard Rustin, and by the writings of existential philosopher Albert Camus, initiated a voting rights campaign deep in the heartland of segregationist defiance, McComb County, Mississippi. Moses belonged to a growing cadre of activists in the Student

Nonviolent Coordinating Committee (SNCC) and in the Congress on Racial Equality (CORE) eager to confront both segregation and the extreme caution of the Kennedy administration in advancing civil rights. They began, in the summer of 1961, with the Freedom Rides that ultimately forced the president and his brother, Attorney General Robert F. Kennedy, to implement the Supreme Court's *Boynton v. Virginia* (1960) ruling prohibiting segregation in interstate travel. SNCC and CORE focused increasingly on restoring African American voting rights. In the autumn of 1961 Moses penned a note from a freezing drunk-tank in Magnolia, Mississippi, where he and eleven others were being held for the crime of attempting to register black voters. "This is Mississippi," he wrote, "the middle of the iceberg. This is a tremor in the middle of the iceberg from a stone that the builders rejected."

Over the next three years, Moses, Stokely Carmichael, Diane Nash, John Lewis, Bob Zellner, and thousands of black and white activists took the civil rights struggle to the heart of the segregationist South: to McComb, Jackson, and Philadelphia, Mississippi; to Albany, Georgia; and to Birmingham and Selma, Alabama. By filling county jails and prison farms, by facing fire hoses, truncheons—and, for Jimmie Lee Jackson, Herbert Lee, Andrew Goodman, James Chaney, Michael Schwerner, and others, by giving their lives—they ultimately made segregation and disfranchisement untenable. In alliance with the more cautious, though equally determined, activists of the Southern Christian Leadership Council and the NAACP, and eventually with the support of the administration of a southern-born president, Lyndon B. Johnson, SNCC and CORE eventually shattered the iceberg of segregation. The 1964 Civil Rights Act and the 1965 Voting Rights Act transformed America. So too did the 1965 Immigration and Nationality Act, which extended the same nondiscriminatory principle to immigration, ended the system of quotas favoring northern Europe, and ushered in new waves of immigration from Latin America, Asia, and Africa.

The nation into which Barack Obama was born was simply not a genuine democracy, and certainly not one in which a person of color might reasonably aspire to the presidency. Nonetheless, by the time he was four or five years old, such a hope, though still wildly audacious, was no longer an impossible dream—even for a boy born in Honolulu to a black Kenyan father and a white mother from Kansas. (We should take with more than a grain of salt, however, Hillary Clinton's claim during their heated primary contest that the fact that Obama as a kindergarten student in Indonesia had written an essay titled 'I Want to Be President'—an obscure fact dredged up by her campaign researchers—*proved* he had harbored a lifelong ambition for the Oval Office.)

HONOLULU, JAKARTA, LOS ANGELES, NEW YORK

While the beaches of Honolulu were more than just five thousand miles away from the back roads of the Mississippi Delta or the shotgun shacks of the Carolinas, the young Barack Obama was not untouched by the dramatic changes wrought by the black freedom struggles, both in America and elsewhere. Indeed, his very existence was to some degree a consequence of those struggles. His father, Barack Hussein Obama Sr., grew up in the small village of Nyangoma-Kogelo in western Kenya, and as a child, herded goats with his father, Hussein Onyango Obama, a domestic servant for British colonial officials. As Barack Obama Jr. would later put it, his grandfather Hussein "had larger dreams for his son," who, first, won a scholarship to study in the capital, Nairobi, and then was selected to participate in a program to educate promising young African students in the United States. The program's founder, the Kenyan nationalist politician and labor leader, Tom Mboya wanted to prepare an African-born elite for government service after the end of British colonial rule, and he looked to America, rather than Britain to do so. To that end, Mboya secured scholarship funds from such civil rights movement stalwarts as Jackie Robinson, Harry Belafonte, and Sidney Poitier. Martin Luther King Jr. and other Montgomery ministers who believed that Africans and African Americans shared a common struggle against colonialism and racism helped fund five of the Kenyan students. (In speeches, Barack Obama has mistakenly credited the family of John F. Kennedy for sponsoring the program that brought his father to America; the Kennedys did provide $100,000 to Mboya's program, but only after Obama Sr. was

already in Hawaii. Other Kenyan students were, however, assisted by the Mboya-Kennedy program, including Africa's first
female Nobel Peace Prize winner, the environmentalist Wan-
gari Maathai.)

A year after arriving at the University of Hawaii at Manoa in
1959, Obama Sr. met Ann Dunham, a white eighteen-year-old
anthropology student born Stanley Ann Dunham in Kansas
and educated at Mercer Island High School on Lake Washington, across from Seattle. Her liberal political inclinations and
protofeminism were encouraged at school by her teachers, at
home by her parents, Stanley Dunham, a gregarious salesman,
and Madelyn Payne Dunham, a somewhat reserved bank em-
ployee, and at the East Shore Unitarian Church in Bellevue,
Washington, known to locals as the "the little Red church on
the hill." At Manoa, Dunham quickly moved into the orbit
of an older group of opinionated, left-leaning graduate and
international students, including the charismatic and politically sophisticated Obama. After Dunham became pregnant,
they married. Interracial marriage was legal in Hawaii, but
was outlawed at that time in twenty-two states. A 1959 Gallup
poll found that 96 percent of white Americans opposed such
unions. As Obama Jr. noted in *Dreams from My Father*, neither
set of parents approved of the marriage, though the opposition
was most intense from Hussein Obama, who "didn't want the
Obama blood sullied by a white woman" (Dreams, 125). The
relationship, complicated by Obama's preexisting marriage to
a woman in Kenya from whom he was separated but not legally
divorced, was short-lived. Obama Sr. left Hawaii for Harvard
to attend graduate school in 1962, and Dunham divorced him
in 1964. Obama Sr. returned to Kenya to work as a government
official. Other than a brief Christmas visit by Obama Sr. to
Hawaii in 1972 when Barack—or Barry as he was known—was
eleven, father and son would never see each other again.

Obama's mother was thus the dominant figure in her son's
formative years. "The values she taught me continue to be
my touchstone when it comes to how I go about the world of
politics" (Jones). Those values were largely secular, though
grounded in the church-based idealism of the early 1960s civil
rights movement. As her son later recalled, it was a fairly ro-
manticized idealism. But there was nothing romantic in Dun-

ham's determination, while still only in her twenties, to raise her son, and to pursue her studies. Assisted by her parents and government food stamps, she completed her undergraduate degree at the University of Hawaii, where she met her second husband, Lolo Soetoro, an Indonesian student.

Obama moved with his mother to Soetoro's home near Jakarta in 1967 and would live in Indonesia for the next four years. He is thus the first American president raised in a predominantly Muslim country—the world's largest—as well as the first president since Herbert Hoover born to a non-American citizen. In Indonesia, Obama, a self-described "little Jakarta street kid," spent joyous days chasing chickens and running from water buffalo, and first heard the Muslim call to prayer, which he has called "one of the prettiest sounds on Earth at sunset" ("Obama: Man of the World," *New York Times* March 6, 2007; *Audacity*, 274). Contrary to claims later made by his political opponents, however, he did not attend an Islamic madrassa. He was enrolled, first, in a Roman Catholic elementary school and then in the state-run Basuki school, which taught children of all faiths—Christians, Buddhists, and Confucians, as well as Muslims. The language of instruction was Indonesian. Obama's most intense schooling, however, came from his mother's exacting 4:00–7:00 A.M. tutorials for English-language correspondence courses before he left for Basuki. Ultimately, his mother's belief that her son would receive a better education in America prompted his return to Hawaii in 1971, where he won a scholarship to attend the Punahou School in Honolulu, an elite preparatory school. Dunham briefly moved back to Hawaii with her daughter (with Lolo), Maya, to live with Obama and her parents, before returning to Indonesia to pursue an anthropology degree on peasant blacksmithing in Java. She later worked with development organizations in Pakistan and Indonesia to set up microfinance programs to help women in remote villages gain access to credit. Dunham's passionate commitment to education, social justice, and grassroots organizing undoubtedly influenced her son's future career path. Her independence, intellectual certainty, and occasional self-righteousness likewise shaped his personality (Scott, "A Free-Spirited Wanderer").

Although she often returned to Hawaii, Dunham's absence from her son's daily life (and his from hers) left a significant void at a time when the teenage Obama was beginning to examine his own racial identity. He outlines this process in *Dreams from My Father* with great honesty and, although it was clearly a time of much anxiety, not a little wit. Barry Obama was, after all, a teenager growing up in the 1970s with black skin, a white mother; a half-Caucasian, half-Indonesian half-sister in Java; and an absent, unknown African father in Kenya. And he lived with aging white Midwestern grandparents in Hawaii, the nation's most ethnically diverse, and only predominantly Asian state. But at the end of his process of self-discovery, and notwithstanding his love for his white mother and grandparents, the physiological fact of his black skin proved to be the most important element in his psychological understanding of self.

Obama's search for a usable African American historical past was abetted by his friendship with the few black students at the ninety-percent-white Punahou School and by his immersion in the works of the major African American intellectuals who struggled with many of the same issues of identity and double consciousness that so troubled him. Yet, while appreciating their genius, the teenage Obama despaired that, despite W. E. B. Du Bois's learning, James Baldwin's love, and Langston Hughes's humor, each of these writers was forced to withdraw, "in the same weary flight, all of them exhausted, bitter men, the devil at their heels" (*Dreams*, 86). The *Autobiography of Malcolm X* provided Obama with a clearer, less angst-ridden model of self-understanding and self-creation, but, unlike Malcolm, he could not wish that his "white blood" be expunged. For all that his parents' marriage was short-lived, Obama had little doubt that, unlike Malcolm's, his own dual heritage was conceived in love, not violence.

Another significant influence was an "old poet," a black drinking buddy of his grandfather's, who had also grown up near Wichita, Kansas, and who is referred to only as "Frank" in *Dreams from My Father*. The historian Gerald Horne has speculated that Frank, who tutored the young Obama in the history of civil rights and other progressive struggles, may have been Frank Marshall Davis, a poet and radical journalist in Chicago in the 1930s and 1940s where he was active in the leftwing National Negro Congress, and was a contemporary of several prominent progressive African American intellectuals, including Langston Hughes, Richard Wright, Paul Robeson, and Margaret Walker. One of the first critics to discuss jazz as a political as much as a cultural and aesthetic phenomenon, jazz exemplified to Davis a distinctive black, working-class challenge to white claims of racial superiority. His poetry and criticism would have a significant influence on the Black Arts Movement of the 1960s. Davis, a Kansas native, moved to Hawaii in the late 1940s on the advice of Paul Robeson and worked as a journalist on a newspaper for the International Longshore and Warehouse Union, one of the most powerful unions on the islands. During the 2008 presidential election, the Obama campaign denied that "Frank" was Frank Marshall Davis when right-wing bloggers tried to use Obama's alleged connection to Davis and Davis's links to the Communist Party as "proof" of Obama's "hidden radical agenda."

Whether "Frank" was Marshall Davis, or not, by 1979, on the eve of leaving Honolulu for university on the mainland, Obama had rejected the old poet's belief that university was "an advanced degree in compromise," or a trap for young black men (*Dreams*, 97). Eighteen-year-old Barry Obama remained unsure, exactly, what college was for when he arrived at Occidental College, a small liberal arts college in Los Angeles in 1979. But by the time he left two years later to complete his bachelor's degree at Columbia University in New York, he had developed a stronger and more balanced sense of his racial identity, an emerging interest in political activism, and a new name—his given name: Barry became Barack.

At both Occidental and Columbia, Obama was active in student politics, notably in antiapartheid protests, where he first discovered the power of his own oratory. As his interest in basketball, drinking, partying, and recreational drugs waned, his devotion to academic study waxed. At Columbia he lived a monk-like existence in small, uncluttered apartments, and absorbed himself in books on political theory, philosophy, international politics, and literature. During that time he also began to write fiction and keep a journal, developing some of the ideas and themes that later appear in *Dreams from My Father*. And it was while Obama was in New York, in 1982, that he learned that his father had died in a car crash in Kenya. Obama Sr. was forty-six.

Obama graduated from Columbia in 1983 with a BA in political science, having developed a vague notion that he might become a community organizer, although he was not entirely sure just what it was that a community organizer did. He did, however, have a romantic image, perhaps in grainy black-and-white, picked up from his mother and his old poet friend Frank, and from books and documentaries of the civil rights struggle. They were stoic, short-haired, neatly dressed black students sitting in at a segregated lunch counter. Or dungaree-wearing SNCC workers like Bob Moses or Stokely Carmichael, leaning on a dusty porch in Mississippi, trying to persuade sharecroppers to take a chance and register to vote. Or defiant children singing freedom songs in crowded southern jails and the streets of Birmingham, braving Bull Connor's attack dogs and fire hoses. Later in the 1980s, after reading *Parting the Waters*, Taylor Branch's magisterial nine-hundred-page history of "America in the King Years" from 1954 to 1963, Obama told a friend, "This is my story."

Rejected by every major civil rights organization he applied to work for, however, including Harold Washington, the recently elected black mayor of Chicago, Obama settled for a job as a researcher and writer for a Manhattan consulting firm, the Business International Corporation. In *Dreams from My Father*, Obama's work for a consulting firm provides a warning of the shallowness of a corporate career, despite its undoubted financial advantages. His fellow employees from that time have suggested, however, that Obama exaggerates the degree to which the company symbolized rapacious 1980s capitalism, perhaps to portray his community organizing career as a more self-sacrificing choice than it actually was.

But it was the general atmosphere of Manhattan, rather than simply its corporate excesses that Obama rejected when he decided to leave the city in 1985. In a revealing passage in *Dreams*, Obama recalls attending a lecture at Columbia by the former SNCC activist Stokely Carmichael, now known as Kwame Ture (spelled Touré in the book). Obama depicts the meeting as dispiriting, full of accusations and counter-accusations of brainwashing and irrelevant debates about

Trotskyism. The progressive left of the 1980s, Obama realized, was no less shallow than the capitalist right. Believing that easy sloganeering and posturing had replaced the certitude and rectitude of SNCC and CORE in the early 1960s, Obama contemplated abandoning his goal of community organizing. The mid-1980s heyday of Reaganism was a time of retrenchment in the American labor movement, when industrial firms in the North closed their gates and reopened in the nonunionized South or in Mexico. It was also a time of growing rates of poverty, drug addiction, and gun violence in America's inner cities—hardly the most propitious decade to be a community organizer. But it was also a time when such work was most desperately needed. So when a rumpled white labor activist approached him to organize black and white steelworkers facing factory closures in the Midwest in the summer of 1985, Obama accepted the $12,000 salary, loaded his belongings into his Honda, and moved to Chicago.

CHICAGO AND HARVARD

Even as Obama had gained a stronger, less conflicted sense of his racial identity during his time in Los Angeles and New York, his understanding of self remained unconnected to place. In neither city did he find an anchor, a community where he could "put down stakes and test my commitments" (*Dreams*, 115). He would find that community and sense of place in Chicago, and especially on its South Side, the largest, most populous collection of African American neighborhoods in the country. Chicago, the "black metropolis" that sociologists St. Clair Drake and Horace R. Cayton portrayed in a ground-breaking study by that title (1945). Chicago, the home of Richard Wright, Margaret Walker, and the Chicago Black Renaissance, the Chicago Giants of Negro League baseball, of Louis Armstrong's Hot Seven, of Chess Records, and the Chicago blues.

Chicago was also the home to people-centered, community-based organizing, which was born after World War II in the theories and programs of Saul Alinsky. Perhaps best known as the author of *Rules for Radicals*, a classic primer on grassroots organizing, Alinsky influenced a host of civil rights and New Left radicals in the 1960s, from SNCC and CORE workers in the South, to the Students for a Democratic Society (SDS) in the Midwest, to César Chávez and others organizing migrant worker organizers in California. In 1969, a Wellesley senior named Hillary Rodham wrote her senior thesis on Alinsky. On the South Side, the twenty-thousand-member Woodland Organization, begun in the early 1960s by Arthur Brazier, a black Pentecostal minister, stood as one of the most successful practical applications of Alinsky's theories. The Developing Communities Project, which employed Obama from 1985 to 1988, followed the Alinsky principles that leaders listen, that change comes from the bottom up, and that ordinary people can do extraordinary things. Those were also the values of grassroots civil rights organizers like Ella Baker and Bob Moses, and they would become Barack Obama's principles as well.

During his first three years in Chicago, Obama achieved some modest success in mobilizing hundreds of residents in the South Side neighborhoods of Roseland and Altgeld Gardens. The skinny kid nicknamed "baby face" helped launch a local job training bank and led protests that forced the city to begin removing asbestos and lead paint from schools and public housing. He also encouraged alliances among black, white, and Hispanic community organizations to stop plans that would have expanded a landfill into wetlands near residential neighborhoods. Obama's fellow organizers from this time have praised his single-minded focus on his community work, and unwillingness to draw attention to himself—an early incarnation of what became known in his 2008 campaign as "No Drama Obama." Others, however, notably Chicago Congressman Bobby L. Rush, have criticized him for taking too much credit for the asbestos removal victory at Altgeld Gardens and for ignoring the efforts of neighborhood residents who began a similar campaign before Obama arrived. Obama was less successful, however, in one of his other projects, a plan to unite 150 of Chicago's black ministers and their congregations to help spearhead community organizing in the city. He was quickly disabused of this notion by his experiences with black ministers who jealously guarded their prerogatives and congregations. Even the Reverend Jeremiah Wright, whose Trinity United Church of Christ was one of the most progressive congregations in the city (and the church where Obama would eventually become a committed Christian), assured Obama that his goal was naive in the extreme, and lacking an appreciation of the often fractious history of the black church. " 'Oh, that sounds real good, Barack. But you don't know Chicago. Man, these preachers in Chicago. You are not going to organize us. No, no, no. Not going to happen'" (Mendell, 69).

Obama's political ambitions also took sharper focus during his first spell in Chicago, which coincided with Harold Washington's term as the city's first black mayor (1983–1987). In an interview with the *Chicago Reader* in 1995, Obama described Washington as "the best of classic politicians. He knew his constituency; he truly enjoyed people." He criticized Washington and his allies, however, for merely "maintaining and working the levers of power." Washington's charisma and hard work gave African Americans their fair share of city services and opportunities long denied by City Hall, but the "potentially powerful collective spirit that went into supporting him"—the coalition of blacks, Hispanics, and progressive whites—was "never translated into clear principles, or into an articulable agenda for community change" (De Zutter).

With ambitions of becoming a future Chicago mayor who might translate those principles into such an agenda, Obama applied to several law schools. In 1988, he was accepted by Harvard Law. Vowing to return to Chicago and community organizing after graduation, he left for Massachusetts, choosing to live not in Cambridge itself, but instead in a basement apartment in the nearby working-class, multi-ethnic city of Somerville. In his first year he worked as an editor on the *Harvard Civil Rights–Civil Liberties Law Review*, and impressed members of the faculty with his maturity and common sense as well as his breadth of knowledge. Lawrence Tribe, the Law School's preeminent expert in constitutional law, has described Obama as one of the most talented students he has ever taught, and relied on him for analytical and research assistance on his November 1989 *Harvard Law Review* article, "The Curvature of Constitutional Space: What Lawyers Can Learn from Modern Physics."

In his senior year, Obama was elected the first African American president of the prestigious (and fiercely competitive) *Harvard Law Review*. (Obama was not the first African American to serve as president of a law review. That honor went to Clara Burrill Bruce, the daughter-in-law of former black U.S. senator Blanche K. Bruce, who presided over the *Boston University Law Review* in 1925). Fellow editors on the *Law Review* have highlighted how Obama's equanimity of temperament served him well in the position. "No-drama Obama," even then, he was able to mediate and even resolve the fractious intellectual and ideological debates between left and right within the *Law Review*. Obama never hid his own political liberalism, however. He continued his active opposition to apartheid and support for affirmative action, and also spoke in favor of African American professor Derrick A. Bell Jr., who resigned from the law school in 1989 to protest Harvard's poor record in granting tenure to minorities. Obama nonetheless earned the respect of political conservatives on the *Law Review* for acting as an honest broker between warring factions. Indeed, he was more likely to be criticized by some on the left, including some of his fellow African American students, for not pursuing a more radical agenda. Such traits would serve him well in his future political career.

After graduating from Harvard Law in 1991, Obama turned down several offers of clerkships for federal judges, the typical next step for former editors of Ivy League law reviews. Instead he returned, as promised, to Chicago. There he spearheaded voter registration efforts that helped secure the 1992 election of Democratic presidential candidate Bill Clinton. His work for Project Vote helped add 150,000 new registrants to the electoral rolls—many of them in black and Hispanic neighborhoods—and also helped elect Carol Moseley Braun, Illinois's first African American U.S. senator and the first black woman and first black Democrat elected to that body. Following the election, and until 2002, Obama served as an associate attorney with Miner, Barnhill & Galland, the leading public interest law firm in Chicago, which also had strong political connections in the city. Judson Miner had been an important white liberal ally of Harold Washington. From 1993 to 2004, Obama also taught courses on constitutional law at the University of Chicago.

In October 1992 Obama married Michelle Robinson, a Chicago native and fellow Harvard Law graduate and attorney he had met while an intern at Newton Minow's law firm, Sidley Austin, during his first summer break from Harvard. The couple had two daughters, Malia, born in 1998, and Natasha, known as Sasha, born in 2001. Obama's marriage to a woman born in working-class South Side Chicago provided the strong sense of rootedness to place and community that he had longed for since his peripatetic childhood and adolescence. As a bonus, Michelle Robinson gave Obama important political connections as well. Her family was well-known and regarded on the South Side, and she had attended school with Santita Jackson, daughter of the Reverend Jesse L. Jackson (and sister of U.S. Representative Jesse Jackson Jr.). Her fellow alumni from Princeton and Harvard Law would later be a useful source of funds for Obama's political campaigns. Finally, Michelle Obama's work as an aide to Mayor Richard M. Daley undoubtedly helped her husband win friends and influence the right people in Chicago's Democratic Party.

Daley's increasingly strong grip on Chicago politics forced Obama to rethink his plans to be mayor of Chicago one day, and persuaded him to pursue another political path, through the Illinois state legislature. Shortly before he won election to that body, Obama published *Dreams from My Father* (1995) a memoir about his unique background as the child of an African father and a white mother from Kansas and his childhood in Hawaii and Indonesia. The book also examines his student experiences and 1980s work as a community organizer in the Chicago. It ends with his journey to the land and extensive family of his father in Kenya, his discovery of his father's unsuccessful and tragic life following his return from America, and with Obama's own reconciliation of his Kenyan and Kansan heritages. A graceful meditation on identity, family, and politics, *Dreams from My Father* enjoyed several positive reviews, notably in the *New York Times*, but it did not generate great sales until its reprinting after Obama's breakthrough election victories in 2004. *Dreams from My Father* has been reprinted many times and has sold over two million copies in hardcover and paperback. Obama's second book, *The Audacity of Hope* (2006), has also gone through many reprintings and has sold over three million copies in hardcover and paperback.

FROM SPRINGFIELD TO WASHINGTON

The luster of Obama's fame as the first African American president of the *Harvard Law Review*, his work as a civil rights lawyer and constitutional law professor, as well as his obvious political and rhetorical skills undoubtedly set him apart from the general pack of Chicago political hopefuls. In 1996 he won a seat representing the 13th district in the Illinois Senate. The 13th encompassed the worlds of both "Obama the University of Chicago Law Professor"—liberal, wealthy, integrated and cosmopolitan Hyde Park—and "Obama the community organizer"—the district's poorer, heavily African American South Side neighborhoods where Jesse Jackson's Operation Breadbasket was located. The election also showed Obama's steely determination to succeed in the seamier precincts of Chicago politics, as well as in the slightly less cutthroat world of the faculty lounge. He had launched his bid for the legislature after the incumbent, Alice Palmer, had stepped down to pursue a seat in the U.S. Congress. When she failed in that effort and tried, with the support of established local black leaders, to reclaim the seat she had relinquished, Obama refused to back down. He also demanded an investigation of questionable signatures on the petitions required for her candidacy, and succeeded in having enough struck off to keep Palmer off the ballot. Obama won the Democratic primary unopposed, which in the Republican-phobic South Side meant he would win the general election with ease.

Obama's achievements in his first terms in the Illinois legislature (formally known as the Illinois General Assembly), as a very junior member of the minority party, were solid, though not spectacular. He helped craft a law that banned the personal use of campaign money by state legislators and banned lobbyists from giving gifts to lawmakers. He also cosponsored bills to reform the state's welfare program, to establish a state Earned Income Tax Credit and to increase child care subsidies for working-class families. In short, he pursued a pragmatic progressive agenda, very much in line with the policies of the Clinton administration that was in office at the time. Obama's cool demeanor, cerebral approach, and links to Hyde Park liberalism irked some of the established black leaders in Springfield, however. These veterans of the civil rights struggles of the 1960s and 1970s believed that the clearly ambitious Obama had not paid his dues, and needed to wait his turn. As at Harvard, Obama sought out the company of conservative Republicans and moderate downstate Democrats, and crafted harmonious working relationships with all shades of political opinion.

Thomas P. "Tip" O'Neill, Speaker of the U.S. House of Representatives in the 1970 and 1980s, often remarked that "all politics is local." O'Neill was always careful to attend to the interests of the predominantly Irish Catholic voters in Cambridge, first in the Massachusetts House of Representatives, and then in the U.S. House. In the Illinois legislature, Barack Obama faithfully followed O'Neill's creed, balancing the interests of his reform-minded, upper-middle-class constituents in Hyde Park and the South Side's traditional working-class voters. By late 1999, at the age of thirty-eight, Obama had worked and lived in Chicago for fifteen years, even returning there to work during the summer recesses at Harvard Law School. While he enjoyed the intellectual stimulation of teaching constitutional law, and had begun to earn the sometimes grudging admiration of his colleagues in the state legislature, it had become increasingly evident that his political ambitions and the transformative social changes he sought would not be satisfied in Springfield. He would have to expand his definition of "the local."

With the political machine of Mayor Richard M. Daley as deeply entrenched in the Second City in the 1990s as his father Richard J. Daley's had been from the mid-1950s to the mid-70s, Obama abandoned his original goal of emulating Harold Washington as mayor of Chicago, and set his sights on the U.S. Congress. Late in 1999, he launched a bid for the U.S. House seat held by Bobby L. Rush, a four-term incumbent and former Black Panther leader. The district included much of the South Side, was two-thirds black, and the winner of the Democratic Party primary was virtually assured of victory in the general election. The claim that Obama was somehow "not black enough" came to the fore in that 2000 Democratic primary, although it was another of Rush's challengers, the black state senator Donne E. Trotter, who most often leveled that charge, famously attacking Obama in the pages of the *Chicago Reader*, a progressive weekly, as aloof and a "white man in black face" (Mendell, 131). Despite Obama's long residency in Chicago, both his opponents easily pegged him as an outsider, highlighting his Harvard Law degree and his ties to white Hyde Park liberals. In language that foreshadowed a common Republican attack in the 2008 presidential election, Rush told the Reader that Obama had only read about the civil rights movement in books and "went to Harvard and became an educated fool. We're not impressed with these folks with these Eastern elite degrees" (Janny Scott, "In 2000, a Streetwise Veteran Schooled a Bold Young Obama," *New York Times*, September 9, 2007).

President Bill Clinton's backing of Bobby Rush, Obama's relationships with a number of white property developers like Antoin "Tony" Rezko, whose dealings in the South Side were distrusted by working-class blacks in the district, and his endorsement by the reliably Republican *Chicago Tribune* certainly did not help his campaign. But it was Obama's failure to appear on an important legislative vote on stricter gun control a few weeks before the primary that delivered the coup de grâce to his challenge. The vote had been highly relevant to the primary campaign, since it had been called shortly after Rush's own son had been shot and killed, an event that had generated much public sympathy for the congressman. That Obama missed the vote while vacationing in Hawaii ensured that he was pilloried by the press (even in the *Tribune*) as well as by his opponents, and Obama's claim that he had remained in Hawaii to look after a sick daughter was not persuasive. His weak performance in the sole televised debate summed up a disastrous campaign. In that debate, Rush delivered a withering critique of his youthful opponent—again presaging a 2008 Republican attack on Obama's allegedly thin resume—asking of Obama, almost in sorrow as much as anger: "Just what's he done? I mean, what's he done?" (Mendell, 131). On primary day, Obama won a majority of white voters, but Rush defeated him by thirty points overall. The vast majority of African Americans heeded the neighborhood posters that read "I'm sticking with Bobby."

In the final analysis, Obama's defeat was as much a reflection of his opponent's strengths as of his own weaknesses. Rush was a popular congressman with a seventy-percent approval rating and was a hero to many for his thirty years of service to the black community. In American politics, especially in House races, incumbents rarely lose. And Obama clearly raised his profile during the course of the race: beginning with a name-recognition of 11 percent, he ended with 30 percent of the vote. That might have been sufficient to launch a later race against Congressman Danny Davis or Jesse Jackson Jr., both in predominantly African American House seats. But the chances of victory, particularly against Jackson, were remote. As with his loss to Bobby Rush, the power of incumbency and Obama's relative outsider status probably would have doomed his candidacy. For a short while, he considered abandoning politics, doubting "whether some kid from Hawaii named Barack Obama could succeed" in a realm where voters based their judgments on superficial matters such as a candidate's name or family ties, rather than issues.

Yet Obama's historical studies would have also told him that only one sitting member of the U.S. House of Representatives—James A. Garfield—has ever been elected directly to the Presidency. All twentieth-century presidents except Dwight D. Eisenhower, the supreme commander of the Allied Expeditionary Force in Europe during World War II, had previously served either as governor, senator, or vice president. If Obama's political ambitions now aimed as high as the presidency—and, according to his brother-in-law, Craig Robinson, they did—he would first need to do something that only three African Americans had achieved in the twentieth century: be elected to statewide office. (The other three were the aforementioned Edward Brooke [R-MA], Democratic governor L. Douglas Wilder of Virginia, and Carol Moseley Braun.) Fortunately for Obama, Moseley Braun had won election to the U.S. Senate from Illinois in 1992, blazing that particular trail in his home state. Moseley Braun had secured victory by forging a coalition of African Americans in Chicago, middle-class voters, especially women, in suburban Cook County and the state capital of Springfield, and highly educated voters in counties that were home to the state's major universities. As noted above, she had also benefited from the coattails of Bill Clinton's successful presidential run and from the successful Project Vote efforts of the young Barack Obama.

In *The Audacity of Hope: Thoughts on Reclaiming the American Dream* (2006), Obama notes that, "at a minimum," any race for a U.S. Senate seat requires "a certain megalomania" (105). But that is only the first step. In addition to vaulting ambition, a willingness to endure a campaign schedule detrimental to a candidate's health and family life, and a determination to avoid a humiliating defeat (a lesson seared into Obama's consciousness by his loss to Rush), a successful race for statewide or national office depends largely on three principal factors: luck, money, and organization. While the latter two factors would be central to Obama's later victories in the 2008 primary season and general election, the former was undeniably a key reason for his successful 2004 run for the U.S. Senate.

Obama's first stroke of luck was Carol Moseley Braun's decision not to run again for the seat that she had lost narrowly in 1998 to Republican Peter Fitzgerald, a millionaire banking heir. That left Obama as the leading African American challenger in the Illinois Democratic primary, in part because of shrewd political calculation and organization, as well as luck. Following his 2000 defeat, Obama began to mend fences with fellow black politicians, including Senator Donne Trotter and others who had mistrusted his Hyde Park connections and questioned his African American bona fides. (Bobby Rush, by contrast, remained skeptical until Obama's 2008 presidential run.) Most important was Obama's evolving relationship with Emil Jones, a state senator Obama dismisses in *Dreams from My Father* as an "old ward heeler." Jones, Democratic minority leader when Obama arrived in the Illinois General Assembly in 1996, either had not read the book, or paid little heed to it, no doubt having been called far worse during a long career in Chicago politics that began the year before Obama was born, when he helped deliver Cook County for the Daley machine and John F. Kennedy. Encouraged by Obama's intelligence and willingness to work hard, Jones gave the freshman legislator several key assignments and viewed himself as something of a father-figure—even, with perhaps a trace of irony, as Obama's "godfather." The turning point came in 2002 when the Democrats, long the minority party in the Illinois Senate, became the majority and elected Jones as the first African American majority leader in that body. The position potentially gave Jones the power to serve as kingmaker to any aspiring Democratic politician in the state. By Jones's account, Obama then asked the elder statesman to back his bid for the 2004 Senate race. This Jones did by securing for Obama the chairmanship of the prominent Health and Human Services Committee, when others had more seniority. Jones also encouraged Obama to take the lead in a bill requiring the videotaping of interrogations and confessions in all capital cases legislation. Obama did so with support both from death penalty opponents and the police, a tricky balancing act that highlighted his developing political skills and ability to forge coalitions.

In part because of Emil Jones's endorsement, but also because of his own efforts to reach out to his black state senate colleagues, Obama began his Senate campaign with far more goodwill in the African American community than he'd enjoyed in his earlier House race. He gained the endorsement of black congressmen Danny Davis and Jesse Jackson Jr., for whom Michelle Obama had once babysat. Indeed, Michelle Obama's South Side bona fides would prove invaluable in laying to rest the belief first aired in the Bobby Rush race that her husband was somehow "not black enough." The long established black radio station WVON, known in its 1940s heyday as the "Voice of the Negro," also provided early support and publicity.

Obama also secured the backing of a handful of white state senate colleagues and worked hard to secure endorsements from established white political leaders, notably Newton N. Minow, the former head of the Federal Communications Commission under John F. Kennedy, and from the well-respected former Illinois U.S. senator Paul Simon. Minow, in whose law firm Obama and Michelle had met, was an unabashed fan, declaring of Obama that he had both a "first-class intellect and a first-class temperament" (Mundy). (Minow's praise was a variation of a half-compliment attributed to the great jurist Oliver Wendell Holmes Jr., who said of President Franklin Roosevelt, "A second-class intellect. But a first-class temperament!") Senator Simon, an unabashed Truman-Kennedy liberal who had run for president in 1988, enjoyed strong support from conservatives in his native southern Illinois and served as something of a role model for Obama's outreach to conservative whites by his policy of "disagreeing without being disagreeable." Although Simon died just before the 2004 Senate primary, he had already made clear his appreciation for Obama's talents and intelligence. A television commercial featuring Simon's daughter endorsing Obama as the heir to her father was used to great effect in his campaign.

Money, the oil of all modern political campaigns, began to trickle in, at first from black business leaders, but eventually from several wealthy, white "Lakefront Liberals," including Penny Pritzker, a businesswoman and philanthropist (and an heiress to the Hyatt hotel fortune). As in his alliance with Emil Jones, Obama's choice of David Axelrod as campaign manager was a politically savvy move that revealed a readiness to mix it up in hardball Illinois politics. Axelrod, a successful political consultant with close ties to the Richard M. Daley administration, had also worked on Paul Simon's successful 1984 U.S. Senate bid. As a former journalist for the *Tribune*, Axelrod had deep ties to journalists and other media figures and professional politicians throughout the state.

By getting Axelrod on board, Obama had shown his seriousness of purpose, but he still had an uphill climb in securing the Democratic nomination for U.S. Senate. That he did so was a mixture of luck and courage. Luck came in the form of a crowded field in the Democratic primary, where he faced only one other African American candidate (a relative newcomer with no institutional support) and two white heavyweight candidates, Blair Hull, a multimillionaire stock trader who financed his own campaign, and Dan Hynes, a well-connected state comptroller favored by many party officials and several unions, who would split the white vote. Hull spent his way to an early lead in opinion polls, but shortly before polling day the release of court records alleging that he had abused his wife dealt a grave blow to his campaign. Ironically, Obama was also helped by his future presidential rival, U.S. Senator John McCain, whose 2002 campaign finance law (coauthored by Wisconsin Democrat Russ Feingold) included a "millionaire's amendment," a provision whereby the rivals of candidates such as Hull could raise up to six times the normal campaign limit of $2,000 per donor. Obama showed courage as the only major candidate in the field who had opposed the Iraq War from its inception—and said so publicly. At an antiwar rally in Chicago

in October 2002, he had made clear that he was no knee-jerk
pacifist, that he did not oppose all wars, but that he did oppose
the war then being hatched against Iraq in neoconservative
think tanks and in the Bush White House. The Iraq venture of
George W. Bush and his strategist, Karl Rove, was, in Obama's
view, "a dumb war. A rash war. A war based not on reason but
on passion, not on principle but on politics" (Crowley, p. 14).
By early 2004, with a rising death toll and a failure to find Iraq's
weapons of mass destruction that were the alleged casus belli
of the invasion, a growing number of Democrats were beginning to turn against the war. Obama's prescience on that issue
undoubtedly brightened his appeal among younger and liberal
whites in the primary, and his progressive credentials helped
win the endorsement of the important left-leaning teachers
and public service employees unions.

The campaign was also a remarkably clean one, devoid
of negative advertising. In the wake of the Al Qaeda terrorist attacks of September 11, 2001, Obama had feared that his
surname might become less of a mild curiosity and more of a
political liability. But none of his opponents made that charge,
partly because they feared alienating black voters. (He would
not be so fortunate four years later.) Much to the surprise of
the political world, Obama would in fact win a relatively easy
primary victory with 53 percent of the vote, more than twice
that of his closest rival, Dan Hynes. The implosion of Hull's
campaign following the revelations about his marriage did
not, as Obama had feared, result in Hull's predominantly
white support shifting to Hynes. Instead, Hull's relatively
independent-minded backers appear to have given their votes
to Obama, the fresh face, rather than to Hynes, the choice of
the party establishment. In the final weeks of campaigning,
Obama's profile was undoubtedly raised by a series of upbeat
television commercials crafted by David Axelrod in which the
candidate first declared (despite initial reluctance) the slo-
gan, "Yes, we can!" In Chicago TV markets these ads pitched
Obama as the heir to Harold Washington; in the rest of the
state they highlighted his endorsement by Paul Simon.

Obama won only 13 of the state's 102 counties, but his margins in Cook County (Chicago), in the suburban "collar counties," and in the state's university towns were substantial. He

won about a quarter of the vote in the rural and small-town counties in the rest of the state, a more than respectable showing by a Chicago-based African American, but evidence, nonetheless, of potential weakness in the general election, since those rural counties were also reliably Republican. That weakness might have been exploited by a formidable Republican candidate, but the winner of the Republican primary in Illinois, businessman Jack Ryan, dropped out of the race following a sex scandal. The Illinois Republican Party turned to Alan Keyes, a former diplomat in the Ronald Reagan administration. Keyes, an African American, was an effective communicator and a spiky debater, who matched Obama's Harvard Law degree with a PhD from the same college. But Keyes had no tangible connection to Illinois, had never held elective office, and had won few votes in his run for the Republican presidential nomination in 2000. Even by the standards of the modern Republican Party, he was an ultraconservative fundamentalist Christian with little appeal to the suburbanites and moderate swing voters who were usually pivotal in Illinois elections. Keyes, in Obama's memorable phrase, came off as a cross between a black Pentecostal preacher and William F. Buckley. Keyes's campaign attacks on Obama went nowhere, but his claims that his opponent was a Marxist, a non-Christian, and not really black because he lacked a slave heritage would be echoed in his future campaigns.

THE 2004 DNC SPEECH
THE LAUNCHING OF THE AMERICAN CANDIDATE

Obama's bid for the Senate also benefited from the reaction to his keynote address to the 2004 Democratic National Convention in Boston. His very selection by the Democratic nominee, Senator John Kerry of Massachusetts, was testament to David Axelrod's efforts to raise his candidate's national profile. And, as in his race for the U.S. Senate, Obama's Harvard connections proved invaluable. Lawrence Tribe, Obama's mentor at the Harvard Law School, advocated for him with Bob Shrum, a top Kerry strategist. Tribe, supremely confident of his former student's intellectual abilities, was less certain of Obama's rhetorical skills. Some in the Kerry campaign worried that

Obama had never used a teleprompter before. Neither need have worried.

Obama was not the first African American to give a DNC keynote address. Texas Congresswoman Barbara Jordan broke that color line in 1976, and gave a speech ranked by 140 scholars of rhetoric as the fifth-greatest American speech of the twentieth century (bettered only by Martin Luther King Jr.'s "I Have a Dream" speech, the inaugural addresses of John F. Kennedy and Franklin D. Roosevelt, and FDR's declaration of war on Japan following Pearl Harbor). Obama's 2004 address probably eclipsed Jordan's in terms of craft. Its impact, certainly, eclipsed that of any previous keynote, transforming an unknown state senator, a "skinny kid with a funny name," into a national political leader of the first rank. The speech also launched many of the themes that would propel Barack Obama into the White House a little more than four years later. Most significantly, his keynote established Obama as a profoundly *American* politician, and arguably as the most representative American candidate ever to seek the presidency. And it was, undoubtedly, a speech that made clear Obama's intention one day to seek that office. Its little more than 2,300 words are, therefore, worthy of some detailed analysis.

Like Barbara Jordan in 1976, Obama began with the improbability of his appearance before the DNC. He announced himself as the son of an immigrant father from Kenya, who grew up herding goats and went to school in a tin roof shack. "Through hard work and perseverance," Obama told his audience, "my father got a scholarship to study in a magical place, America, that shone as a beacon of freedom and opportunity to so many who had come before." In a few well-crafted lines, Obama appealed not only to two pillars of his party—people of color and immigrants of all colors—but also laid claim to the "up by your bootstraps" mantle of Booker T. Washington and the Horatio Alger stories of yore. By invoking his mother's Kansas roots, he reached out deftly to voters in the rural Midwest, where the prairie populism forged in the agrarian depressions of the 1880s and 1930s had been eclipsed by the Republican Party's adoption of a "family values" populism. By highlighting his Kansas grandfather's work on farms and oil rigs in the Depression and his service in Patton's army in World War II, Obama both hailed and staked a family claim to the dignity of labor and the patriotism of working-class men of "the Greatest Generation." By praising his grandmother for raising his mother while working on a bomber assembly line, he acknowledged the importance of women's patriotism as well as the dignity of *their* labor—in both senses of that word. Obama also made clear that his appearance on that stage was also the consequence of federal government action, specifically the Democratic New Deal and Fair Deal policies of Franklin Roosevelt and Harry Truman: "After the war, they studied on the G.I. Bill, bought a house through FHA, and later moved west all the way to Hawaii in search of opportunity." After expressing "gratitude for the diversity of my heritage," Obama returned to situate himself in a no less profoundly American tradition, that of American exceptionalism. "I stand here knowing that my story is part of the larger American story, that I owe a debt to all of those who came before me, and that, in no other country on earth, is my story even possible." In a shade over four hundred words, Barack Obama had introduced himself to America and to the world.

The middle of his speech was somewhat more prosaic, though still compelling. A few lines were crafted to appeal to Illinois voters—he had an election to win after all. Thus Obama gave shout-outs to the voters in the collar counties around Chicago who did not want their tax money wasted by either welfare agencies or the Pentagon; recounted a conversation with a (presumably Irish American) patriotic G.I. named Seamus he had met "in a V.F.W. Hall in East Moline, Illinois"; and declared, "If there is a child on the South Side of Chicago who can't read, that matters to me, even if it's not my child." Obama then moved beyond the local to a celebration of "the true genius of America," namely, "a faith in simple dreams, an insistence on small miracles." These "small miracles" include the expectation that our children should be fed and safe; "that we can say what we think, write what we think, without hearing a sudden knock on the door"—a constitutional law professor's gentle but powerful rebuke of the erosion of civil liberties by the Bush administration's USA Patriot Act—and "that our votes will be counted—at least most of the time," a crowd-pleasing reminder that the U.S. Supreme Court halted the Florida recount in the 2000 election, thereby delivering the presidency to George W. Bush.

Obama's words undoubtedly resonated with Democratic partisans in the Boston convention center, and he made clear that John Kerry and the Democrats would best allow Americans to "pursue our individual dreams and yet still come together as one American family." But the overall arc of his speech was decidedly post-partisan. "There is not a liberal America and a conservative America, he declared, "there is the United States of America. There is not a black America and a white America and Latino America and Asian America—there's the United States of America." Obama urged his fellow citizens to look beyond the divisive politics that had characterized the 1990s and, but for a moment of national unity following the attacks of September 11, 2001, much of the first decade of the twenty-first century as well. "The pundits like to slice and dice our country into Red [Republican] States and Blue [Democratic] States," he told the watching millions.

> But I've got news for them, too. We worship an awesome God in the Blue States, and we don't like federal agents poking around in our libraries in the Red States. We coach Little League in the Blue States and yes, we've got some gay friends in the Red States.... We are one people, all of us pledging allegiance to the Stars and Stripes, all of us defending the United States of America.

Ultimately, he argued, the 2004 election came down to a simple question: Do we participate in a politics of cynicism, or do we participate in a politics of hope? In answering for the latter choice, Obama's oratory shifted away from invocations of the American civic religion found in the Declaration of Independence and in the national motto of "E Pluribus Unum" inscribed on the Great Seal of the United States, to language rooted in the prophetic tradition of the African American church. Indeed, in his rising cadences, he began for the first time in his speech to adopt the soaring rhetoric that most Americans, black, white, and others, traditionally expect of black politicians. Driven by a "righteous wind," Obama's commitment to "the audacity of hope" unabashedly evoked the dreams of Martin Luther King Jr. and others in the 1960s, and Jesse Jackson, who had kept hope alive in the 1980s. The words, however, came from another Chicago pastor—his own—the Rev. Jeremiah Wright. Those words found their musical complement in the gospel choir that immediately followed his speech, urging those watching to "keep on pushing!" "The next day," an article in the *New York Times* began, "Barack Obama owned the town" (Randal C. Archibold, "Day After, Keynote Speaker Finds Admirers Everywhere," *New York Times*, July 29, 2004).

While his keynote performance stunned many observers, and relieved his own and Kerry's advisors, there was one individual who was not surprised: Obama himself. On the evening of his speech, and with trademark self-confidence, he predicted to a Chicago journalist that he would deliver a slam-dunk. Referring to LeBron James, then the rising star in the National Basketball Association, Obama told the journalist, "I'm LeBron, baby! I can play on this level. I got game." (Mendell, 2).

After his DNC speech, Obama's general election battle against Keyes was anticlimactic. That November, Obama won an easy victory, with 70 percent of the vote. The voters of Illinois had (again) elected an African American to the Senate, and that alone would have made him a figure of major national importance. Obama's compelling DNC address, however, had also made him a genuine star in the firmament of the Democratic party—a commodity that would be much in demand following Kerry's narrow defeat by Bush and the growing unpopularity of the war in Iraq.

As the Senate's only African American member and as a senator from one of the nation's largest states, Obama immediately emerged as a rising star in a Democratic Party that had suffered a second straight (and narrow) defeat in the presidential elections in 2004, albeit this time at the ballot box rather than in the U.S. Supreme Court. In *The Audacity of Hope* Obama elaborated on the themes of hope and national unity that were central to his convention keynote address. Sales from the book and from a reissued *Dreams from My Father* enabled him to join the ranks of most of his Senate colleagues, who were millionaires. The cultural phenomenon of Obamamania, and his "crossover appeal" beyond the traditional confines of black politics, drew comparisons with his fellow black Chicagoan, the talk show host and media mogul

Oprah Winfrey, as well as with the nation's first Roman Catholic president John F. Kennedy. His life story, which embraced the Kansas heartland of his mother and the African immigrant experience of his father, was to some degree exotic, but it was also increasingly typical in a nation where, as of the 2000 census, non-Hispanic whites were already in the minority in four states, including Obama's native Hawaii and the nation's most populous state, California.

Because he was now involved in a national campaign, many of the issues about his name, identity, and blackness that Obama had dealt with in Chicago and Illinois politics were raised again in a national context. The African American journalist and critic Debra J. Dickerson argued in Salon.com, for example, that Obama was "not black" because he was not a descendant of slaves brought to America from Africa and, like a Nigerian-born cab driver in Harlem, "had no part in our racial history." Rather, Obama and the cab driver were "Americans of African immigrant extraction." Yet the answer of many blacks (and indeed, others) to Dickerson's analysis was, generally, so what? There have historically been differences and tensions, too, between lighter- and darker-skinned blacks; between West Indian immigrants (also the descendants of slaves) and American blacks; and between northern and southern people of color. George Schuyler, an iconoclastic black journalist raised in Syracuse, New York, often remarked with pride that his family had never lived in the South and had never been slaves, but, as he and Obama would both learn, such distinction mattered little to whites. "A black person learns very early," Schuyler wrote in his autobiography, "that his color is a disadvantage in a world of white folks. This being an unalterable circumstance, one also learns to make the best of it" (*Black and Conservative* [1966], 1). Or, as Obama once put it, New York cab drivers who ignore his efforts to hail a taxi somehow fail to recognize his white Kansan side.

Moreover, Obama's election symbolized a broader generational shift in African American politics. Black political gains in the 1970s, 1980s, and 1990s were largely achieved by a generation of politicians who came of age in the southern civil rights movement, or in urban Democratic politics. Obama was only one of several young Ivy League–educated black politicians who came to prominence in the early 2000s. In 2002, Artur Davis (Harvard Law) was elected to the U.S. House from Alabama. Three years later, another Harvard Law graduate—and also a close friend of Obama's—Deval Patrick, was elected governor of Massachusetts, while in 2006 Cory Booker (Yale Law and Queen's College, Oxford) and Michael Nutter (University of Pennsylvania) were elected mayors of Newark and Philadelphia, respectively. Congressman Harold Ford Jr., a Penn grad (and the son of a U.S. congressman) who preceded Obama as a DNC keynote speaker, came close to winning a U.S. Senate race in Tennessee the same year. Patrick and Nutter were slightly older than Obama; Davis, Booker, and Ford a few years younger. All are generally progressive pragmatists and are less partisan than earlier generations of black politicians, although Ford, chairman of the Democratic Leadership Council, and Artur Davis have been more willing to adopt socially as well as economically conservative positions in order to broaden their appeal as possible statewide candidates in the South.

THE AMERICAN CANDIDATE
THE 2008 PRESIDENTIAL ELECTION

Even after the upsurge in outbreak of Obamamania in 2005 and 2006, Obama's decision to enter the 2008 Democratic race for the presidency still surprised many observers. His February 2007 announcement, outside the State Capitol building in Springfield, brought to mind the last Illinois native to win the presidency, Abraham Lincoln. But it was also a reminder that Obama had been a middle-ranking state legislator in Springfield a mere three years earlier. And that no successful presidential candidate since Lincoln had less executive or legislative experience. In the U.S. Senate, Obama was ranked ninety-eighth out of a hundred in seniority. His legislative achievements were slim. As at Harvard Law School and in the Illinois legislature, he forged close relationships with Republicans, working with the conservative senator Tom Coburn of Oklahoma to improve transparency in government operations. More substantively he teamed up with the moderate GOP veteran Dick Lugar of Indiana, a former chairman of the Senate Foreign Relations Committee, to expand America's role in helping the nations of the former Soviet Union eliminate conventional weapons stockpiles and detect and interdict weapons of mass destruction. Seasoned Capitol Hill observers speculated, however, that Obama was not a Senate natural. Unlike New York's Hillary Rodham Clinton, the favorite for the Democratic nomination, he chafed at the endless loop of committee and subcommittee meetings.

Obama worked tirelessly at town hall meetings back home with his Illinois constituents and at fund-raising events for fellow Democrats grateful for his star power. But he resented the amount of time spent away from his wife and growing children, who remained in Chicago. The twenty-month marathon of a presidential campaign would, of course, place an even greater strain on any candidate's family life. And, for African American presidential candidates, there was the added burden of the fear of assassination, a fear that persuaded Alma Powell, wife of General Colin Powell, to veto her husband's consideration of a possible bid for the presidency in 1996 and 2000, when opinion polls indicated he might be elected, either as a Republican or an independent. When Michelle, Malia, and Sasha Obama gave their assent to his candidacy in late 2006, Obama's presidential campaign began in earnest.

Obama recognized that some might view his candidacy as precocious, but declared in his Springfield announcement that he was driven by what Martin Luther King Jr. had called "the fierce urgency of now." It was a nice phrase, but he had felt the same urgency in his 2000 race against Bobby Rush, and had lost soundly. Moreover, after the November 2006 midterm elections handed both houses of Congress back to the Democrats, and with the plummeting approval ratings of President Bush following the inept and immoral federal response to Hurricane Katrina (August 2005), Obama's main Democratic rivals shared that same sense of urgency and possibility. In addition to their equally keen ambition, all of them had considerably more experience than Obama. Chris Dodd of Connecticut chaired the Senate Banking Committee; Joe Biden of Delaware, a senator since 1973, chaired the Senate Foreign Relations Committee and had previously chaired Judiciary. Both Hillary Clinton and former North Carolina senator John Edwards had both experienced presidential races, Clinton in her husband's successful 1992 and 1996 bids, and Edwards during his own presidential bid and as John Kerry's running mate in 2004. All were, like Obama, centrist Democrats on domestic affairs, although Edwards had developed a more aggressive populist stump speech and persona than had been evident in his one term in the Senate. Little separated the candidates on foreign affairs, either, with one major exception: Obama had been a clear and consistent opponent of the Bush administration's rationales for invading Iraq, whereas his main rivals had all supported a 2002 Senate resolution authorizing an expansive, unrestricted use of force against Saddam Hussein's regime.

John Kerry's narrow loss in the 2004 election (48 percent to Bush's 51) indicated the growing concerns of American voters that the Bush administration had misled the country to war on dubious claims of Iraq's possession of weapons of mass destruction. Throughout 2005 and 2006, as American and Iraqi casualty rates rose higher, as daily carnage made Iraq appear on the brink of civil war, and as Bush's already fragile "coalition of the willing" dwindled to his own administration and Britain's prime minister Tony Blair, Obama's skepticism on the war appeared increasingly prudent. By getting the most important foreign policy decision of the twenty-first century wrong, the much-vaunted Capitol Hill "experience" of Dodd, Clinton, Biden, and Edwards lost much of its luster.

Drawing partly on small donations raised through the Internet (building on the successful methods pioneered by Democratic presidential candidate Howard Dean in 2003 and 2004) and partly on larger donations solicited by Penny Pritzker and others who had funded his Senate bid, Obama's campaign amassed $140 million between January 2007 and January 2008. This gave him a slight financial edge over the expected Democratic favorite, Hillary Clinton of New York. A tight, disciplined grassroots campaign organization propelled Obama to victory in the first race of the presidential season, the Iowa caucuses. Given Iowa's relatively small black population, his path to victory came through the overwhelming support of young white voters and university graduates, and from party activists opposed to the Iraq War. Most remarkably, on a snowy January night, 250,000 turned up to caucus, double the normal turnout and nearly three times the figure that the

Clinton campaign had anticipated. By winning in America's heartland with 38 percent—and in a state that had voted for George W. Bush in 2004—it would become much harder for Obama's rivals to portray him as anything other than a mainstream American candidate.

Clinton, who placed third in Iowa with 29 percent, close behind John Edwards at 30, rallied to win the following New Hampshire primary by three points, largely on the basis of strong support from women voters and older, working-class white Democrats. Because New Hampshire was also a largely white state, the next primary, in South Carolina where half of the Democratic voters were African American, would provide the first real test of black voting opinion. For months it had seemed that, as happened with Obama's failed challenge to Bobby Rush, black voters would prefer the candidate they had long known and trusted. In several opinion polls prior to the Iowa caucuses, Obama trailed Clinton among African Americans, largely because of black loyalty to Bill Clinton's administration, but also because of Hillary's own strong links to the black community. Clinton also enjoyed the endorsements of several leading black Democrats in Congress, notably representatives Charles Rangel of New York and John Lewis of Georgia, a veteran of SNCC and symbol of the civil rights movement. Obama's victory in Iowa proved to blacks in South Carolina and other states, however, that he could win white votes and thus the Democratic nomination. In the January 28 South Carolina primary Obama won the vast majority of black votes (78 percent to Clinton's 19). He also won a respectable minority among whites, again performing particularly well among younger voters and those with college degrees. Obama won South Carolina with 55 percent of the vote, over Clinton with 27 and John Edwards with 18.

The patterns set in Iowa, New Hampshire, and South Carolina largely shaped the contests that followed. Both Obama and Clinton raised unprecedented sums of money—forcing even the wealthy trial lawyer John Edwards to drop out (after his disappointing third-place finish in South Carolina, the state where he was born). Obama's fund-raising exceeded Clinton's, however, and the New York senator was forced to lend several million dollars of her own money to keep her campaign afloat. Obama performed best in western and Plains caucus states largely ignored by Clinton, where his campaign developed a strong ground game and where Obama's background as a community organizer proved to be invaluable in face-to-face, door-to-door campaigning. (The Clinton team did not have a clear grasp of how caucuses worked and had dithered about whether to even compete in Iowa—as Bill Clinton had not in 1992. Her strategists had expected to blow away the competition by Super Tuesday and had not formulated a long-term strategy.) Obama also won primaries in the former confederate states of Virginia, Alabama, Louisiana, and Mississippi, where blacks formed between a third and a half of the Democratic electorate. Clinton performed best in northeastern primary states and in California and Texas, where her stronger name recognition and superior Hispanic support assured victory. In nearly all states, but especially in the East, Clinton enjoyed a clear edge among two of the most important voting blocs in the Democratic primary: white women and voters over sixty-five years of age. The two shared the spoils of the twenty-two state races on Super Tuesday in early February, but eleven straight primary and caucus victories later that month propelled Obama to a comfortable delegate lead over Clinton.

Obama's momentum was stalled, however by a media frenzy in March 2008 over comments made by his pastor, Rev. Jeremiah Wright. Some of Wright's incendiary remarks, made in the wake of the September 11, 2001, terrorist attacks, were construed by many commentators, especially on the right and in the Clinton campaign, as anti-American. Played on a seemingly endless loop on cable news and the Internet (especially on YouTube), Wright was seen at Trinity United Church of Christ, declaring "God damn America!" and asserting that the 9/11 attacks were the chickens of U.S. foreign policy come home to roost (echoing the figure of speech Malcolm X used after the Kennedy assassination).

Obama faced the controversy head-on in a speech he called "A More Perfect Union," given at the National Constitution Center in Philadelphia. (See Appendix.) As with his 2004 DNC speech, Obama wrote the address by himself, and, as *The New Yorker's* Hendrik Hertzberg has noted, made the risky choice of "treat[ing] the American people as adults capable of complex thinking." Regarding Wright's comments, Obama stated that he could no more disown the pastor than he could disown the black community, or his own white grandmother, whom he deeply loved, but who had "uttered racial or ethnic stereotypes that made me cringe." Using the speech as a teaching moment, he encouraged nonblack Americans to understand the historical context of the black experience in America that shaped Reverend Wright's worldview. To simply wish the anger of Wright and others away, Obama argued, "to condemn it without understanding its roots, only serves to widen the chasm of misunderstanding that exists between the races." And likewise, he asked people of color to appreciate the "legitimate concerns" of whites who opposed affirmative action or busing, and whose fears of inner-city crime were not necessarily rooted in racism. Americans, he concluded could continue to view race as a spectacle, as in the O. J. Simpson trial, or as a tragedy, as in the aftermath of Hurricane Katrina. Or they could begin to move beyond "a racial stalemate we've been stuck in for years" in pursuit of a more perfect union in which Americans of all races worked together to confront their mutual problems of affordable health care, a growing housing crisis, and the war in Iraq. A few commentators noted that it was self-serving for Obama to suggest that America could overcome its past of racial division by uniting behind his candidacy, but on the whole his speech was well received, and appeared to stanch the bleeding to his support caused by his pastor's comments.

The Wright controversy did not end there, however. In late April, before the National Press Club in Washington, Wright again blamed the September 11 attacks on the consequence of American policies and praised Nation of Islam leader Louis Farrakhan. He also stated his belief that the U.S. government had deliberately invented the AIDS virus as a means of genocide against minorities, citing the government's admitted role in allowing the Tuskegee syphilis experiment to continue for decades. Shortly afterward, Obama condemned these comments unequivocally and ended his twenty-year relationship with Wright and Trinity Church.

Another controversy followed Obama's comments at a San Francisco fund-raiser prior to the Pennsylvania primary in April, when he stated of working-class white voters facing hard economic times that "it's not surprising that they get bitter, they cling to guns or religion or antipathy to people who aren't like them or anti-immigrant sentiment or anti-trade sentiment as a way to explain their frustrations" (Fowler). In the wake of these comments and Clinton's creative—and surprisingly successful—efforts to recreate herself as a guntotin,' Crown Royal–swiggin' gal from her grandpa's hometown of Scranton, Obama lost the Pennsylvania primary. The loss provoked much media speculation about his problems as an elitist with an intractable problem with white working-class voters. That argument, eagerly pursued by the Clinton campaign, gained some traction with her landslide victories in West Virginia and Kentucky. But it was undermined by subsequent Obama victories in North Carolina (by 15 percent, with relatively strong white, as well as overwhelming black support), a late-night, narrow loss in Indiana (49.3 percent to Clinton's 50.7), and again by 15 percent in the predominantly white state of Montana, where he continued to show strong appeal to western voters. Clinton's electability argument was also hampered by the fact that not once in the Democratic primaries had she ever led Obama in total delegates.

At the formal end of the caucus and primary season on June 3, 2008, Obama became the first African American to secure the nomination of a major national party. According to the Associated Press, his final margin on that date exceeded Clinton's by 125 pledged delegates from primaries and caucuses, but swelled to 300 with the addition of votes cast by remaining Democratic party leaders, the so-called "superdelegates." Both candidates won around 18 million votes. Four days after Obama was hailed the presumptive nominee of his party, Senator Clinton conceded defeat and endorsed his candidacy. Obama's six-month contest against Hilary Clinton was the longest, closest, most exciting, and first truly national, party campaign in American political history. That Senator Clinton continued her challenge to the bitter end, though seen as potentially divisive at the time, ultimately strengthened Obama's general election chances. For, had Obama wrapped up the nomination early by winning New Hampshire and one of the big Super Tuesday primary states, as well as Iowa and South Carolina, he probably would not have registered as many new voters or identified as many potential donors, both in states like Virginia and North Carolina, where he won, or in Ohio, Pennsylvania, and Indiana, where he made a strong showing.

Despite fears that the long, divisive primary season—and the frustrated ambitions of the Clintons and their supporters—might continue into the Democratic National Convention in Denver, Colorado, in August, the Convention proved to be remarkably harmonious. Both Hillary and Bill Clinton provided strong endorsements of Obama's candidacy, and his choice of the experienced Delaware senator Joseph R. Biden Jr. as his running mate was viewed as a sensible, serious pick. In his speech to the Convention, Bill Clinton praised the choice: "...in his first presidential decision, the selection of a running mate, he hit it out of the park." Obama's acceptance speech, delivered on the forty-fifth anniversary of King's 1963 "I Have a Dream" address to the March on Washington, was given before an ecstatic crowd of 84,000 at Mile High Stadium in Denver. Most print and television pundits graded the speech a success, and the morning after, a Gallup daily tracking poll gave Obama a clear eight-point cushion over his Republican rival, Senator John McCain of Arizona.

That same day, however, McCain's choice of Alaska governor Sarah Palin as his vice-presidential running mate stole some of Obama's thunder and probably reduced the traditional opinion poll "bounce" most candidates enjoy after conventions. Despite the Clintons' endorsement of Obama, there was some initial indication that former Clinton supporters, particularly women, might be persuaded to vote for McCain and the Republicans' first-ever female vice-presidential candidate. Palin, a right-wing conservative firmly opposed to all forms of abortion, even in the cases of rape and incest, also helped McCain with the some of the evangelical "values" voters who had backed George W. Bush but had never warmed to McCain, even though he was also anti-choice. Gradually, however, most of the Clinton-supporting women who briefly considered the selection of Palin as a reason to vote for McCain backed off once her right-of-the mainstream positions became known. Ultimately, however, Palin also proved to be an ill-prepared and woefully inexperienced candidate—before serving as governor for only twenty months she was the mayor of a small town outside Anchorage—thus undercutting McCain's original campaign premise that Obama, as only a first-term U.S. senator, was a risky presidential choice.

Commentators generally agreed that, in addition to the Palin issue, four key factors shaped Obama's victory. First, he ran a campaign unmatched by any Democrat in recent memory, both in terms of its disciplined message and the unity of its staff. Second, after foregoing federal matching campaign funds, Obama raised a record $640 million by October 15, 2008—half from individual contributions under $200—giving him a significant advantage in television advertising and in creating an extensive get-out-the vote strategy. Third, voters clearly preferred Obama's economic policies, particularly after the banking and stock market crises that broke in the last month and a half of the campaign. Obama, surrounded by former Treasury and Federal Reserve officials, appeared calm and steady, while the purportedly more experienced Republican candidate appeared erratic, impulsive, and not well versed in economic matters. McCain's charge that Obama's policies represented "socialism" and that he would be a "redistributor in chief" persuaded few voters, partly because Obama succeeded in hammering home the promise that he would cut taxes for 95 percent of Americans, and also because his tax policies would only rescinded the same Bush tax cuts for families earning more than $250,000 that McCain had opposed in 2001. The fourth key to Obama's success was somewhat under the radar of the mainstream media (Tim Dickinson, "The Machinery of Hope," *Rolling Stone*, March 20, 2008). At the Republican convention former New York City mayor Rudolph Giuliani and Sarah Palin had both sneered at the notion of a former community organizer thinking he was qualified to be president, but the joke was on them. Obama's campaign combined Internet savvy (helped by a founder of the social networking web site Facebook) with an extensive grassroots network of enthusiastic volunteers who trained field organizers at "Camp Obamas" around the country and directed e-mail and cell phone–driven get-out-the-vote efforts far exceeding anything his opponents had imagined possible.

Another strategic difference from previous campaigns was that the Obama team did not write off the South or other "red" regions where Republicans had previously held sway. Obama was impressed by DNC chairman Howard Dean's "fifty-state strategy" of competing in every state in the union—with paid staff and field offices—an approach many Democratic Party powers had resisted. In addition, the campaign planned a variety of avenues to rack up enough electoral college votes that an Obama victory would not depend on a win in Ohio or Florida as in 2000 and 2004. Again, the hard work of competing in the primaries paid dividends. Obama pushed hard in the last days of the campaign, urging his supporters not to let up for a single second—and Democrats, paranoid and burned by the two previous lost elections, heeded his call and worked hard to get out the vote.

On November 4, 2008, Barack Obama became the first African American elected to the U.S. presidency, defeating John McCain by an electoral vote margin of 365–173 and by 53 to 46 percent of the popular vote, where he won 67 million votes to McCain's 58 million. The magnitude of that victory, and its meaning for African Americans, in particular, was perhaps best captured on election night when television cameras focused their lenses on Jesse Jackson, the revered and sometimes controversial Civil Rights veteran and two-time candidate for the Democratic nomination for president, standing in a crowd in Chicago's Grant Park with tears streaming down his cheeks, overwhelmed at the culmination of centuries of struggle by African Americans, a day that so many gave so much to achieve, and which so many never lived to see.

And yet, beyond that wondrous and inescapable achievement, Obama's victory also has resonance for America as a whole. Contrary to a claim in one of John McCain's campaign ads, an analysis of the 2008 election results suggests that Obama was the "American candidate that Americans were waiting for." In a less than subtle way, McCain's commercial implied that Obama was somehow foreign, not American, or at any rate not a *real* American *from* real America, as Sarah Palin put it. The McCain-Palin campaign tried several variations on this theme, depicting him as a celebrity, an elitist, as someone who "pals around with terrorists," and, finally and quaintly, as a radical socialist. Like Hillary Clinton's hesitant admission that Obama was not a Muslim, "as far as I know," none of these efforts to depict Obama as an "other" quite stuck. And they did not stick because Obama's policies, his character, and his values were at least as close to the mainstream of American public opinion as those of his opponents. Obama, a quintessentially American candidate, was, after all, born and raised in the farthest West, and educated in California and the Northeast. He made his home in a Midwestern city home to hundreds of thousands of black southern migrants; the southern civil rights movement shaped his core political values and philosophy; and his large margins in southern states propelled him to victory in the 2008 primaries.

An analysis of his general election win likewise suggests that Obama built one of the most broad-based, diverse, and national coalitions of voters since World War II. His tally of at least 67 million votes was not only greater than any previous American candidate, but it was the largest total won in any democratic election for a head of state in the world. (The head of state of India, the world's largest democracy, is elected indirectly.) He was the first Democrat since Jimmy Carter in 1976 to win a majority of the vote; Bill Clinton won only a plurality of the vote in 1992 and 1996, as did Al Gore in 2000, although George W. Bush's won that year's election because of his plurality on the Supreme Court. (Clinton in 1992 was running against two opponents, George H. W. Bush and H. Ross Perot.) Among *all* Democratic presidents since the party's founding nearly two centuries ago, only three—Lyndon Johnson (1964), FDR (1932, 1936, and 1940), and Andrew Jackson (1828 and 1832)—ever won more than Obama's 53 percent share of the total vote. In 1944, FDR also secured 53 percent, on the eve of the Allied victory in World War II.

In terms of geography and demography, Obama also defied the conventional wisdom. And he did so with a vice-presidential running mate from Delaware—the first time the Democrats had won an election without a southerner on the ticket since World War II. Despite the claims of pundits who said the 2000 and 2004 elections had revealed an enduring cleavage between a Republican majority in the "heartland" and South and a permanent Democratic minority on the coasts and industrial Midwest, Obama won states in every region of the country. He secured all the states John Kerry won in 2004, flipped

Iowa and Ohio in the Midwest, recaptured several states that Bill Clinton had won in the 1990s, Florida in the South, New Mexico, Nevada, and Colorado in the West, and added North Carolina, which last voted for a Democratic in 1976, as well as Virginia and Indiana, which had been solidly Republican states since Obama was a toddler. Only in Appalachia, the Ozarks, and Oklahoma—the country music belt where Clinton defeated him soundly in the primaries—did Obama lose ground compared to John Kerry's run four years earlier.

According to a national exit poll of 16,000 voters, Obama won a higher percentage of the male vote than any Democrat since 1964, although he remained just shy of a majority. (http://elections.nytimes.com/2008/results/president/exit-polls.html). His 56 percent share of the women's vote was two points higher than Clinton's (1996) and Gore's (2000), and Obama also restored the traditional Democratic advantage among Roman Catholics and Hispanics, groups that had gone to George W Bush in 2000 and 2004. Among African Americans he won an unprecedented 95 percent of the vote. Despite some rather implausible efforts by Republicans to portray Obama as a friend of Hamas and "weak" on Israel, he won 78 percent of Jewish voters. The national exit poll did not survey America's 3.5 million Muslims, but one analysis indicates that Obama won 89 percent of the Muslim vote.

The youth vote (18–29 year olds) increased by more than 2.2 million between 2004 and 2008, and Obama won two-thirds of that demographic, the greatest youth margin in history by a considerable distance. He also won a majority among whites under 30. McCain only won a majority among people over 65, rural and small-town voters, evangelical Protestants, and all whites. Each of these groups represented a declining share of the national population, particularly whites who in 2008 constituted less than three-quarters of the electorate for the first time. By contrast, 90 percent of the electorate was white in 1964, the year before the landmark Immigration Act which, as noted above, led to a dramatic increase in immigration from Latin America, Asia, and Africa, notably in the states won by Obama in 2008. Indeed, just as it became commonplace to argue that Lyndon Johnson's 1965 Voting Rights Act "delivered the South to the Republican Party for a generation," by identifying the Democrats as the party of blacks and civil rights, so may we now view Johnson's 1965 Immigration Act as the catalyst for delivering the West to the Democrats by greatly increasing the number of Asians and Hispanic voters in that region.

Yet, for all that slicing and dicing of the electorate, as Obama might put it, the most important factor shaping his election victory was the economy. Three-fifths of all voters named the economic crisis as the most pressing issue facing the nation; 60 percent of those voters backed Obama. At the time of writing, it is not clear whether Obama's victory marks a distinctive partisan realignment in America, such as occurred in 1932 under Democrat Franklin Roosevelt, or in 1980 under Republican Ronald Reagan. But in the broad historical context, there can be little doubt that Obama's victory gives him the clearest mandate of any Democratic president since Lyndon Johnson, particularly since his party also made gains in the U.S. House and Senate. How Obama uses that mandate will determine whether he joins Roosevelt and Reagan as transformative presidents.

The rest of the world is also anxious to see how and whether the son of a Kenyan, raised and educated for four years in Indonesia, will reshape America's relationship with the wider world. Barack Obama has the advantage of taking office after eight years in which the United States largely ignored the views of its allies, as well as of its enemies, particularly on Iraq, but also on matters of trade, global warming, and the creation of an International Criminal Court. After the Bush years, the bar for success is set exceedingly low, but the expectations of foreign countries may also be too high. A Gallup opinion poll covering seventy-three countries and half of the world's population, released just before the November election, revealed that citizens outside the United States supported Obama over John McCain by a margin of 3 to 1. That figure rose to 8 to 1 in several African countries, including Kenya. Only in the former Soviet republic of Georgia, where John McCain had forthrightly supported that country in its August 2008 standoff with Russia, and where Obama had been more even-handed, did citizens of a foreign country support the Republican. Perhaps the most significant result came, however, from

Palestine, where only 16 percent of respondents thought the election of either candidate would make a difference to their country. Seventy-two percent of Palestinians stated that the election of either candidate would make no difference to their country and to their daily lives. In no other country was there such pessimism about the American "change" election. We might measure the success of an Obama presidency, then, on whether a politician with a talent for building consensus can increase the optimism of Palestinians, as well as of Israelis, toward American foreign policy. And, indeed, on whether an Obama presidency succeeds in giving citizens in the Middle East, Iraq, Afghanistan, Sudan, the Democratic Republic of the Congo, and other nations beset by war and genocide, poverty, and disease, the audacity to hope.

★ ★ ★ ★

BIBLIOGRAPHY

Becker, Jo, and Christopher Drew. "Pragmatic Politics, Forged on the South Side." *New York Times*, May 11, 2008.

Branch, Taylor. *Parting the Waters: America in the King Years, 1954–63.* New York: Simon and Schuster, 1988.

Carson, Clayborne. *In Struggle : SNCC and the Black Awakening of the 1960s.* Cambridge, Mass.: Harvard University Press, 1981.

Chappell, David L. *A Stone of Hope: Prophetic Religion and the Death of Jim Crow.* Chapel Hill: University of North Carolina Press, 2004.

Crowley, Michael. "Cinderella Story: Is Obama's Iraq Record Really a Fairy Tale?" *New Republic*, February 27, 2008.

Davis, Frank Marshall. *Livin' the Blues: Memoirs of a Black Journalist and Poet.* Edited by John Edgar Tidwell. Madison: University of Wisconsin Press, 1992.

De Zutter, Hank. "What Makes Obama Run?" *Chicago Reader*, December 8, 1995. http://www.chicagoreader.com/obama/951208/

Dickerson, Debra J. "Colorblind: Barack Obama would be the great black hope in the next presidential race—if he were actually black." Salon.com, January 22, 2007. http://www.salon.com/opinion/feature/2007/01/22/obama/index.html

Dickinson, Tim. "The Machinery of Hope." *Rolling Stone*, March 20, 2008. http://www.rollingstone.com/news/coverstory/19106326

Dougherty, Steve. *Hopes and Dreams: The Story of Barack Obama.* New York: Black Dog & Leventhal, 2007.

Drake, St. Clair, and Horace R. Cayton. *Black Metropolis: A Study of Negro Life in a Northern City, 1945.* Rev. ed., with an introduction by Richard Wright and a new foreword by William Julius Wilson. Chicago: University of Chicago Press, 1993.

Fowler, Mayhill. "Obama: No Surprise That Hard-Pressed Pennsylvanians Turn Bitter." *Huffington Post*, April 11, 2008. http://www.huffingtonpost.com/mayhill-fowler/obama-no-surprise-that-ha_b_96188.html.

Gates, Henry Louis, Jr. "In Our Lifetime." theroot.com, Nov. 5, 2008. http://www.theroot.com/id/48731

Grossman, James R., *Land of Hope: Chicago, Black Southerners, and the Great Migration*. Chicago: University of Chicago Press, 1989.

Hertzberg, Hendrik. "Obama Wins." *New Yorker*, November 17, 2008.

Horne, Gerald. "Rethinking the History and Future of the Communist Party." *Political Affairs*, March 28, 2007.

Horne, Gerald. *The White Pacific: U.S. Imperialism and Black Slavery in the South Seas after the Civil War*. Honolulu : University of Hawai'i Press, 2007.

Jones, Tim. "Obama's Mom: Not Just a Girl from Kansas." *Chicago Tribune*, March 27, 2007. http://www.chicagotribune.com/news/politics/obama/chi-0703270151mar27-archive,0,2623808.story

King, Richard H. *Civil Rights and the Idea of Freedom*. New York: Oxford University Press, 1992.

Kantor, Jodi. "An Effort to Bridge a Divide." *New York Times*, March 18, 2008.

Lemann, Nicholas. *The Promised Land: the Great Black Migration and How it Changed America*. New York: Vintage, 1992.

Lizza, Ryan. "Making It: How Chicago Shaped Obama," *New Yorker*, July 21, 2008. http://www.newyorker.com/reporting/2008/07/21/080721fa_fact_lizza

Mack, Kenneth, and Jim Chen. "Barack Obama Before He Was a Rising Political Star." *Journal of Blacks in Higher Education*, October 21, 2004, 99–101.

Mendell, David. *Obama: From Promise to Power*. New York: Amistad/HarperCollins, 2007.

Mullen, Bill V. *Popular Fronts: Chicago and African-American Cultural Politics, 1935–46*. Urbana: University of Illinois Press, 1999.

Mundy, Liza. "A Series of Fortunate Events." *Washington Post*, August 12, 2007, W10.

Niven, Steven. "Another Tremor in the Iceberg: Barack Obama's Candidacy and the Modern Civil Rights Movement." OUP blog, November 5, 2008. New York: Oxford University Press. http://blog.oup.com/2008/11/president_barack_obama/

Obama, Barack. *The Audacity of Hope: Thoughts on Reclaiming the American Dream*. New York: Crown, 2006.

Obama, Barack. *Dreams from My Father: A Story of Race and Inheritance*. New York: Times Books, 1995.

Olopade, Dayo. "Barack's Big Night." *New Republic*, August 25, 2008. http://www.tnr.com/politics/story.html?id=e6de946c-8b9c-45ca-b9d1-9921b60bdc0a

Powell, Michael. "Embracing His Moment, Obama Preaches Hope in New Hampshire." *New York Times*, January 5, 2008.

Ralph, James R., Jr. *Northern Protest: Martin Luther King, Jr., Chicago, and the Civil Rights Movement*. Cambridge, Mass.: Harvard University Press, 1993.

Samuels, David. "Invisible Man: How Ralph Ellison Explains Barack Obama. *New Republic*, October 22, 2008. http://www.tnr.com/politics/story.html?id=5c263e1d-d75d-4af9-a1d7-5cb761500092

Scott, Janny. "Obama's Account of New York Years Often Differs from What Others Say." *New York Times*, October 30, 2007.

Tayler, Letta, and Keith Herbert. "Obama Forged Path as Chicago Community Organizer." *Newsday*, March 2, 2008.

A MORE PERFECT UNION

BARACK OBAMA

DELIVERED 18 MARCH 2008,
PHILADELPHIA, PENNSYLVANIA

Despite what appeared to be the Obama campaign's strategy, it was perhaps inevitable that the ascendance of an African American to the status of presumptive major-party presidential nominee would lay bare the issues of race and social class in America. Indeed, U.S. Senator Barack Obama had avoided speaking publicly about race for so long that some in the political press had dubbed him the country's first "post-racial" candidate. In March 2008, however, as the long primary contest against former First Lady Hillary Clinton dragged on, race suddenly leapt to the forefront of the national political dialogue. At issue was Obama's twenty-year relationship with Jeremiah Wright, the longtime pastor of Chicago's Trinity United Church of Christ. When video footage surfaced in which Wright, among other pronouncements, appeared to suggest that the United States had brought upon itself the terrorist attacks of September 11, 2001, a media firestorm erupted. Obama was repeatedly asked to renounce Wright's statements and to explain his long association with the church, among Chicago's largest and most influential African American religious and community institutions.

It bears mentioning that much of the controversy over Wright and his sermons was driven by a mainstream media establishment that tended sometimes to overemphasize the contentious remarks of African American religious figures while ignoring (if not tacitly excusing) similar statements from conservative white evangelicals. Wright's sermons were delivered in the boisterous, fiery, sometimes bawdy prophetic style familiar to many African American Christians, but perhaps largely unknown to white audiences. The clips, which appeared first on *ABC News* but spread quickly to the other network and cable news outlets and to online video sources such as YouTube.com, were composed of short, spliced segments that were played, and replayed, without the benefit of context or elaboration. Wright's 9/11 comment, for example, was in fact a quotation from former U.S. Ambassador Edward Peck. His "God damn America" was cut short, too, so that Wright's prophetic condemnation of a country that had wandered away from the path of righteousness ("God damn America for as long as she acts like she is God and she is supreme") was reduced instead to an inflammatory utterance of naked anti-Americanism.

Whatever part played by the national media, however, it soon became apparent that Obama's attempts to distance himself from Wright had failed to quell the controversy. On March 18, 2008, the junior senator from Illinois addressed an audience at Philadelphia's Constitution Center. In his speech, Obama explains his association with Wright and again repudiates many of Wright's statements, before broadening the address to encompass the greater and (for almost all voters) far more relevant issues of race and class. In Obama's estimation, America's march toward a "more perfect union" has reached a "racial stalemate," wherein blacks and whites harbor resentments toward one another but are unable to find a productive means of expressing them. Papering over those resentments, he insists, is precisely the wrong thing to do:

> "But the anger is real; it is powerful; and to simply wish it away, to condemn it without understanding its roots, only serves to widen the chasm of misunderstanding that exists between the races."

Written by Obama himself and delivered in a simple, plain-spoken style, Obama's nearly forty-minute-long address was instantly hailed as one of the most important speeches in a generation on the American racial divide. The speech was widely viewed. Polls taken after the address revealed that a surprisingly large majority of Americans had either seen the speech or were aware of it (despite the fact that Obama delivered his address early in the morning on a workday). The

Obama Campaign's YouTube.com posting of the speech in its entirety quickly rose to more than three million views. Even many conservative commentators, including those hostile to Obama's policy positions, gave voice to their admiration. (One, Douglas Kmiec, a former U.S. Attorney General under both presidents Ronald Reagan and George H.W. Bush, was moved to endorse Obama for president.)

For his part, Reverend Wright would appear again shortly after, making a number of public remarks that ultimately led Obama to issue a personal renunciation of Wright's statements and positions, and to finally break ties with his former pastor. Wright appeared only infrequently—and only in spirit—during the remainder of the presidential cycle. The campaign of the Republican candidate, Senator John McCain of Arizona, had decided the use of Wright against Obama was "out of bounds." Ultimately, Barack Obama seized the presidency with a landslide victory in the Electoral College and a majority of the popular vote, earning a clear national mandate from the American people. Though issues surrounding race relations in the United States will remain salient for the foreseeable future, for at least one moment, Obama managed (perhaps unwillingly) to reintroduce a great many Americans to the idea that those issues are a part of our national life. No one speech, however, nor any one candidate, he cautioned, can heal those old wounds:

> "But it is where we start. It is where our union grows stronger. And as so many generations have come to realize over the course of the 221 years since a band of patriots signed that document in Philadelphia, that is where the perfection begins."

★

"We the people, in order to form a more perfect union."

Two hundred and twenty one years ago, in a hall that still stands across the street, a group of men gathered and, with these simple words, launched America's improbable experiment in democracy. Farmers and scholars; statesmen and patriots who had traveled across an ocean to escape tyranny and persecution finally made real their declaration of independence at a Philadelphia convention that lasted through the spring of 1787.

The document they produced was eventually signed but ultimately unfinished. It was stained by this nation's original sin of slavery, a question that divided the colonies and brought the convention to a stalemate until the founders chose to allow the slave trade to continue for at least twenty more years, and to leave any final resolution to future generations.

Of course, the answer to the slavery question was already embedded within our Constitution—a Constitution that had at is very core the ideal of equal citizenship under the law; a Constitution that promised its people liberty, and justice, and a union that could be and should be perfected over time.

And yet words on a parchment would not be enough to deliver slaves from bondage, or provide men and women of every color and creed their full rights and obligations as citizens of the United States. What would be needed were Americans in successive generations who were willing to do their part—through protests and struggle, on the streets and in the courts, through a civil war and civil disobedience and always at great risk—to narrow that gap between the promise of our ideals and the reality of their time.

This was one of the tasks we set forth at the beginning of this campaign—to continue the long march of those who came before us, a march for a more just, more equal, more free, more caring and more prosperous America. I chose to run for the presidency at this moment in history because I believe deeply that we cannot solve the challenges of our time unless we solve them together—unless we perfect our union by understanding that we may have different stories, but we hold common hopes; that we may not look the same and we may not have come from the same place, but we all want to move in the same direction—towards a better future for of children and our grandchildren.

This belief comes from my unyielding faith in the decency and generosity of the American people. But it also comes from my own American story.

I am the son of a black man from Kenya and a white woman from Kansas. I was raised with the help of a white grandfather who survived a Depression to serve in Patton's Army during World War II and a white grandmother who worked on a bomber assembly line at Fort Leavenworth while he was overseas. I've gone to some of the best schools in America and lived in one of the world's poorest nations. I am married to a black American who carries within her the blood of slaves and slaveowners—an inheritance we pass on to our two precious daughters. I have brothers, sisters, nieces, nephews, uncles and cousins, of every race and every hue, scattered across three continents, and for as long as I live, I will never forget that in no other country on Earth is my story even possible.

It's a story that hasn't made me the most conventional candidate. But it is a story that has seared into my genetic makeup the idea that this nation is more than the sum of its parts—that out of many, we are truly one.

Throughout the first year of this campaign, against all predictions to the contrary, we saw how hungry the American people were for this message of unity. Despite the temptation to view my candidacy through a purely racial lens, we won commanding victories in states with some of the whitest populations in the country. In South Carolina, where the Confederate flag still flies, we built a powerful coalition of African Americans and white Americans.

This is not to say that race has not been an issue in the campaign. At various stages in the campaign, some commentators have deemed me either "too black" or "not black enough." We saw racial tensions bubble to the surface during the week before the South Carolina primary. The press has scoured every exit poll for the latest evidence of racial polarization, not just in terms of white and black, but black and brown as well.

And yet, it has only been in the last couple of weeks that the discussion of race in this campaign has taken a particularly divisive turn.

On one end of the spectrum, we've heard the implication that my candidacy is somehow an exercise in affirmative action; that it's based solely on the desire of wide-eyed liberals to purchase racial reconciliation on the cheap. On the other end, we've heard my former pastor, Reverend Jeremiah Wright, use incendiary language to express views that have the potential not only to widen the racial divide, but views that denigrate both the greatness and the goodness of our nation; that rightly offend white and black alike.

I have already condemned, in unequivocal terms, the statements of Reverend Wright that have caused such controversy. For some, nagging questions remain. Did I know him to be an occasionally fierce critic of American domestic and foreign policy? Of course. Did I ever hear him make remarks that could be considered controversial while I sat in church? Yes. Did I strongly disagree with many of his political views? Absolutely—just as I'm sure many of you have heard remarks from your pastors, priests, or rabbis with which you strongly disagreed.

But the remarks that have caused this recent firestorm weren't simply controversial. They weren't simply a religious leader's effort to speak out against perceived injustice. Instead, they expressed a profoundly distorted view of this country—a view that sees white racism as endemic, and that elevates what is wrong with America above all that we know is right with America; a view that sees the conflicts in the Middle East as rooted primarily in the actions of stalwart allies like Israel, instead of emanating from the perverse and hateful ideologies of radical Islam.

As such, Reverend Wright's comments were not only wrong but divisive, divisive at a time when we need unity; racially charged at a time when we need to come together to solve a set of monumental problems—two wars, a terrorist threat, a falling economy, a chronic health care crisis and potentially devastating climate change; problems that are neither black or white or Latino or Asian, but rather problems that confront us all.

Given my background, my politics, and my professed values and ideals, there will no doubt be those for whom my statements of condemnation are not enough. Why associate myself with Reverend Wright in the first place, they may ask? Why not join another church? And I confess that if all that I knew of Reverend Wright were the snippets of those sermons that have run in an endless loop on the television and You Tube, or if Trinity United Church of Christ conformed to the caricatures being peddled by some commentators, there is no doubt that I would react in much the same way

But the truth is, that isn't all that I know of the man. The man I met more than twenty years ago is a man who helped introduce me to my Christian faith, a man who spoke to me about our obligations to love one another; to care for the sick and lift up the poor. He is a man who served his country as a U.S. Marine; who has studied and lectured at some of the finest universities and seminaries in the country, and who for over thirty years led a church that serves the community by doing God's work here on Earth—by housing the homeless, ministering to the needy, providing day care services and scholarships and prison ministries, and reaching out to those suffering from HIV/AIDS.

★

In my first book, *Dreams from My Father*, I described the experience of my first service at Trinity:

> "People began to shout, to rise from their seats and clap and cry out, a forceful wind carrying the reverend's voice up into the rafters. . . . And in that single note—hope!—I heard something else; at the foot of that cross, inside the thousands of churches across the city, I imagined the stories of ordinary black people merging with the stories of David and Goliath, Moses and Pharaoh, the Christians in the lion's den, Ezekiel's field of dry bones. Those stories—of survival, and freedom, and hope—became our story, my story; the blood that had spilled was our blood, the tears our tears; until this black church, on this bright day, seemed once more a vessel carrying the story of a people into future generations and into a larger world. Our trials and triumphs became at once unique and universal, black and more than black; in chronicling our journey, the stories and songs gave us a means to reclaim memories that we didn't need to feel shame about . . . memories that all people might study and cherish—and with which we could start to rebuild."

That has been my experience at Trinity. Like other predominantly black churches across the country, Trinity embodies the black community in its entirety—the doctor and the welfare mom, the model student and the former gangbanger. Like other black churches, Trinity's services are full of raucous laughter and sometimes bawdy humor. They are full of dancing, clapping, screaming and shouting that may seem jarring to the untrained ear. The church contains in full the kindness and cruelty, the fierce intelligence and the shocking ignorance, the struggles and successes, the love and yes, the bitterness and bias that make up the black experience in America.

And this helps explain, perhaps, my relationship with Reverend Wright. As imperfect as he may be, he has been like family to me. He strengthened my faith, officiated my wedding, and baptized my children. Not once in my conversations with him have I heard him talk about any ethnic group in derogatory terms, or treat whites with whom he interacted with anything but courtesy and respect. He contains within him the contradictions—the good and the bad—of the community that he has served diligently for so many years.

I can no more disown him than I can disown the black community. I can no more disown him than I can my white grandmother—a woman who helped raise me, a woman who sacrificed again and again for me, a woman who loves me as much as she loves anything in this world, but a woman who once confessed her fear of black men who passed by her on the street, and who on more than one occasion has uttered racial or ethnic stereotypes that made me cringe.

These people are a part of me. And they are a part of America, this country that I love.

Some will see this as an attempt to justify or excuse comments that are simply inexcusable. I can assure you it is not. I suppose the politically safe thing would be to move on from this episode and just hope that it fades into the woodwork. We can dismiss Reverend Wright as a crank or a demagogue, just as some have dismissed Geraldine Ferraro, in the aftermath of her recent statements, as harboring some deep-seated racial bias.

But race is an issue that I believe this nation cannot afford to ignore right now. We would be making the same mistake that Reverend Wright made in his offending sermons about America—to simplify and stereotype and amplify the negative to the point that it distorts reality.

The fact is that the comments that have been made and the issues that have surfaced over the last few weeks reflect the complexities of race in this country that we've never really worked through—a part of our union that we have yet to perfect. And if we walk away now, if we simply retreat into our respective corners, we will never be able to come together and solve challenges like health care, or education, or the need to find good jobs for every American.

Understanding this reality requires a reminder of how we arrived at this point. As William Faulkner once wrote, "The past isn't dead and buried. In fact, it isn't even past." We do not need to recite here the history of racial injustice in this country. But we do need to remind ourselves that so many of the disparities that exist in the African American community today can be directly traced to inequalities passed on from an earlier generation that suffered under the brutal legacy of slavery and Jim Crow.

Segregated schools were, and are, inferior schools; we still haven't fixed them, fifty years after *Brown v. Board of Education*, and the inferior education they provided, then and now, helps explain the pervasive achievement gap between today's black and white students.

Legalized discrimination—where blacks were prevented, often through violence, from owning property, or loans were not granted to African American business owners, or black homeowners could not access FHA mortgages, or blacks were excluded from unions, or the police force, or fire departments—meant that black families could not amass any meaningful wealth to bequeath to future generations. That history helps explain the wealth and income gap between black and white, and the concentrated pockets of poverty that persists in so many of today's urban and rural communities.

A lack of economic opportunity among black men, and the shame and frustration that came from not being able to provide for one's family, contributed to the erosion of black families—a problem that welfare policies for many years may have worsened. And the lack of basic services in so many urban black neighborhoods—parks for kids to play in, police walking the beat, regular garbage pick-up and building code enforcement—all helped create a cycle of violence, blight and neglect that continue to haunt us.

This is the reality in which Reverend Wright and other African Americans of his generation grew up. They came of age in the late 1950s and early 1960s, a time when segregation was still the law of the land and opportunity was systematically constricted. What's remarkable is not how many failed in the face of discrimination, but rather how many men and women overcame the odds; how many were able to make a way out of no way for those like me who would come after them.

But for all those who scratched and clawed their way to get a piece of the American Dream, there were many who didn't make it—those who were ultimately defeated, in one way or another, by discrimination. That legacy of defeat was passed on to future generations—those young men and increasingly young women who we see standing on street corners or languishing in our prisons, without hope or prospects for the future. Even for those blacks who did make it, questions of race, and racism, continue to define their worldview in fundamental ways. For the men and women of Reverend Wright's generation, the memories of humiliation and doubt and fear have not gone away; nor has the anger and the bitterness of those years. That anger may not get expressed in public, in front of white co-workers or white friends. But it does find voice in the barbershop or around the kitchen table. At times, that anger is exploited by politicians, to gin up votes along racial lines, or to make up for a politician's own failings.

And occasionally it finds voice in the church on Sunday morning, in the pulpit and in the pews. The fact that so many people are surprised to hear that anger in some of Reverend Wright's sermons simply reminds us of the old truism that the most segregated hour in American life occurs on Sunday morning. That anger is not always productive; indeed, all too often it distracts attention from solving real problems; it keeps us from squarely facing our own complicity in our condition, and prevents the African American community from forging the alliances it needs to bring about real change. But the anger is real; it is powerful; and to simply wish it away, to condemn it without understanding its roots, only serves to widen the chasm of misunderstanding that exists between the races.

In fact, a similar anger exists within segments of the white community. Most working- and middle-class white Americans don't feel that they have been particularly privileged by their race. Their experience is the immigrant experience—as far as they're concerned, no one's handed them anything, they've built it from scratch. They've worked hard all their lives, many times only to see their jobs shipped overseas or their pension dumped after a lifetime of labor. They are anxious about their futures, and feel their dreams slipping away; in an era of stagnant wages and global competition, opportunity comes to be seen as a zero sum game, in which your dreams come at my expense. So when they are told to bus their children to a school across town; when they hear that an African American is getting an advantage in landing a good job or a spot in a good college because of an injustice that they themselves never committed; when they're told that their fears about crime in urban neighborhoods are somehow prejudiced, resentment builds over time.

Like the anger within the black community, these resentments aren't always expressed in polite company. But they have helped shape the political landscape for at least a generation. Anger over welfare and affirmative action helped forge the Reagan Coalition. Politicians routinely exploited fears of crime for their own electoral ends. Talk show hosts and conservative commentators built entire careers unmasking bogus claims of racism while dismissing legitimate discussions of racial injustice and inequality as mere political correctness or reverse racism.

Just as black anger often proved counterproductive, so have these white resentments distracted attention from the real culprits of the middle class squeeze—a corporate culture rife with inside dealing, questionable accounting practices, and short-term greed; a Washington dominated by lobbyists and special interests; economic policies that favor the few over the many. And yet, to wish away the resentments of white Americans, to label them as misguided or even racist, without recognizing they are grounded in legitimate concerns—this too widens the racial divide, and blocks the path to understanding.

This is where we are right now. It's a racial stalemate we've been stuck in for years. Contrary to the claims of some of my critics, black and white, I have never been so naïve as to believe that we can get beyond our racial divisions in a single election cycle, or with a single candidacy—particularly a candidacy as imperfect as my own.

But I have asserted a firm conviction—a conviction rooted in my faith in God and my faith in the American people—that working together we can move beyond some of our old racial wounds, and that in fact we have no choice is we are to continue on the path of a more perfect union.

For the African American community, that path means embracing the burdens of our past without becoming victims of our past. It means continuing to insist on a full measure of justice in every aspect of American life. But it also means binding our particular grievances—for better health care, and better schools, and better jobs—to the larger aspirations of all Americans—the white woman struggling to break the glass ceiling, the white man whose been laid off, the immigrant trying to feed his family. And it means taking full responsibility for own lives—by demanding more from our fathers, and spending more time with our children, and reading to them, and teaching them that while they may face challenges and discrimination in their own lives, they must never succumb to despair or cynicism; they must always believe that they can write their own destiny.

Ironically, this quintessentially American—and yes, conservative—notion of self-help found frequent expression in Reverend Wright's sermons. But what my former pastor too often failed to understand is that embarking on a program of self-help also requires a belief that society can change.

The profound mistake of Reverend Wright's sermons is not that he spoke about racism in our society. It's that he spoke as if our society was static; as if no progress has been made; as if this country—a country that has made it possible for one of his own members to run for the highest office in the land and build a coalition of white and black; Latino and Asian, rich and poor, young and old—is still irrevocably bound to a tragic past. But what we know—what we have seen—is that America can change. That is true genius of this nation. What we have already achieved gives us hope—the audacity to hope—for what we can and must achieve tomorrow.

In the white community, the path to a more perfect union means acknowledging that what ails the African American community does not just exist in the minds of black people; that the legacy of discrimination—and current incidents of discrimination, while less overt than in the past—are real and must be addressed. Not just with words, but with deeds—by investing in our schools and our communities; by enforcing our civil rights laws and ensuring fairness in our criminal justice system; by providing this generation with ladders of opportunity that were unavailable for previous generations. It requires all Americans to realize that your dreams do not have to come at the expense of my dreams; that investing in the health, welfare, and education of black and brown and white children will ultimately help all of America prosper.

In the end, then, what is called for is nothing more, and nothing less, than what all the world's great religions demand—that we do unto others as we would have them do unto us. Let us be our brother's keeper, Scripture tells us. Let us be our sister's keeper. Let us find that common stake we all have in one another, and let our politics reflect that spirit as well.

For we have a choice in this country. We can accept a politics that breeds division, and conflict, and cynicism. We can tackle race only as spectacle—as we did in the OJ trial—or in the wake of tragedy, as we did in the aftermath of Katrina—or as fodder for the nightly news. We can play Reverend Wright's sermons on every channel, every day and talk about them from now until the election, and make the only question in this campaign whether or not the American people think that I somehow believe or sympathize with his most offensive words. We can pounce on some gaffe by a Hillary supporter as evidence that she's playing the race card, or we can speculate on whether white men will all flock to John McCain in the general election regardless of his policies.

We can do that.

But if we do, I can tell you that in the next election, we'll be talking about some other distraction. And then another one. And then another one. And nothing will change.

That is one option. Or, at this moment, in this election, we can come together and say, "Not this time." This time we want to talk about the crumbling schools that are stealing the future of black children and white children and Asian children and Hispanic children and Native American children. This time we want to reject the cynicism that tells us that these kids can't learn; that those kids who don't look like us are somebody else's problem. The children of America are not those kids, they are our kids, and we will not let them fall behind in a twenty-first century economy. Not this time.

This time we want to talk about how the lines in the Emergency Room are filled with whites and blacks and Hispanics who do not have health care; who don't have the power on their own to overcome the special interests in Washington, but who can take them on if we do it together.

This time we want to talk about the shuttered mills that once provided a decent life for men and women of every race, and the homes for sale that once belonged to Americans from every religion, every region, every walk of life. This time we want to talk about the fact that the real problem is not that someone who doesn't look like you might take your job; it's that the corporation you work for will ship it overseas for nothing more than a profit.

This time we want to talk about the men and women of every color and creed who serve together, and fight together, and bleed together under the same proud flag. We want to talk about how to bring them home from a war that never should've been authorized and never should've been waged, and we want to talk about how we'll show our patriotism by caring for them, and their families, and giving them the benefits they have earned.

I would not be running for President if I didn't believe with all my heart that this is what the vast majority of Americans want for this country. This union may never be perfect, but generation after generation has shown that it can always be perfected. And today, whenever I find myself feeling doubtful or cynical about this possibility, what gives me the most hope is the next generation—the young people whose attitudes and beliefs and openness to change have already made history in this election.

There is one story in particularly that I'd like to leave you with today—a story I told when I had the great honor of speaking on Dr. King's birthday at his home church, Ebenezer Baptist, in Atlanta.

There is a young, twenty-three year old white woman named Ashley Baia who organized for our campaign in Florence, South Carolina. She had been working to organize a mostly African American community since the beginning of this campaign, and one day she was at a roundtable discussion where everyone went around telling their story and why they were there.

And Ashley said that when she was nine years old, her mother got cancer. And because she had to miss days of work, she was let go and lost her health care. They had to file for bankruptcy, and that's when Ashley decided that she had to do something to help her mom.

She knew that food was one of their most expensive costs, and so Ashley convinced her mother that what she really liked and really wanted to eat more than anything else was mustard and relish sandwiches. Because that was the cheapest way to eat.

She did this for a year until her mom got better, and she told everyone at the roundtable that the reason she joined our campaign was so that she could help the millions of other children in the country who want and need to help their parents too.

Now Ashley might have made a different choice. Perhaps somebody told her along the way that the source of her mother's problems were blacks who were on welfare and too lazy to work, or Hispanics who were coming into the country illegally. But she didn't. She sought out allies in her fight against injustice.

Anyway, Ashley finishes her story and then goes around the room and asks everyone else why they're supporting the campaign. They all have different stories and reasons. Many bring up a specific issue. And finally they come to this elderly black man who's been sitting there quietly the entire time. And Ashley asks him why he's there. And he does not bring up a specific issue. He does not say health care or the economy.

He does not say education or the war. He does not say that he was there because of Barack Obama. He simply says to everyone in the room, "I am here because of Ashley."

"I'm here because of Ashley." By itself, that single moment of recognition between that young white girl and that old black man is not enough. It is not enough to give health care to the sick, or jobs to the jobless, or education to our children.

But it is where we start. It is where our union grows stronger. And as so many generations have come to realize over the course of the 221 years since a band of patriots signed that document in Philadelphia, that is where the perfection begins.